THE
HIDDEN
GAMES OF
ORGANIZATIONS

THE HIDDEN GAMES OF ORGANIZATIONS

MARA SELVINI PALAZZOLI,
LUIGI ANOLLI, PAOLA DI BLASIO,
LUCIA GIOSSI, INNOCENZO PISANO,
CARLO RICCI, MARICA SACCHI,
AND VALERIA UGAZIO

FOREWORD BY PAUL WATZLAWICK
TRANSLATION BY ARNOLD J. POMERANS

PANTHEON BOOKS NEW YORK

Library of Congress Cataloging-in-Publication Data

Sul fronte dell'organizzazione. English.
  The hidden games of organizations.
  Translation of: Sul fronte dell'organizzazione.
  Bibliography: p.
  Includes index.
  1. Organizational behavior. 2. Psychology, Industrial. I. Selvini Palazzoli, Mara.
II. Title.
HD58.7.S9213   1987   158.7   86-5079
ISBN 0-394-54315-7

Book design by Dana Kasarsky

CONTENTS

FOREWORD

The introductory words "It is a pleasure and a privilege" have become a cliché. And yet, this is what it *is* for me: a pleasure and a privilege to write a foreword to a book whose principal author I met in 1967 and whose brilliant work and friendship I have deeply appreciated ever since. It was in the late sixties that Mara Selvini and her colleagues were becoming interested in Gregory Bateson's work, especially in its application to family therapy. They therefore knew of the work we were doing along these lines at the Mental Research Institute in Palo Alto.

When I first visited her institute in Milan in 1971, the traditional psychiatric framework was still very much the basis of their approach to human problems. By 1972 their work had undergone a total change; and when I consulted with them for the third time, in 1974, I had nothing to contribute anymore: the systemic approach had become the core element of their research and their clinical work.

Seen from the vantage point of 1986, the shift from monadic to systemic thinking seems little more than an obvious development that had already taken place in the natural sciences. But at that time, marked by the impatient awareness of having reached the limits of individual, intrapsychic, introspective, retrospective, insight-oriented views on problem formation and problem resolution, the new paradigm was like a breath of fresh air. There was, first and foremost, the realization that the nature of interaction is *more than and different from* the sum total of the interacting elements and that any attempt to break up this dynamic *gestalt* into its single components had to lead to absurd reifications. We began to see that the puzzling nature of these reifications had so far permitted only *one* explanation, namely that they were unconscious. After all, they defied rational explanation. Now it began to dawn on us that these manifestations were unconscious only in the sense that our traditional views could not make any sense out of them. Systems of human relationships began to reveal themselves as *superpersonal* entities, governed by internal laws and, therefore, beset by "pathologies" of their own, requiring very different techniques of "treatment" than the ones with which we were familiar. Or to put it into less traditional and clinical terms: We became aware of the basic nature of systemic functioning and its processes, be it in a system as small as the relationship between two spouses, or as large as a business corporation or a government agency.

Another surprising discovery was that a system's stability—its *order*—is possible only at the price of a certain degree of internal *disorder*. As long as this disorder stays within tolerable limits or is somehow defined as acceptable or even desirable, the system is likely to stay viable and functioning. However, as clinical work with family systems shows, other forms of systemic stability may be maintained only at the expense of great discomfort—usually a so-called psychiatric condition—to one of its members, the identified patient. What is fascinating for those of us engaged in organizational research and management consulting is that there, too, this realization now begins to prevail; that is, that problems existing or arising within the organization are not necessarily the result of the incompetence of one person, but may be of that superpersonal, systemic quality mentioned earlier.

The scientific disciplines and other sources that constitute the basis of this perspective are too numerous to be mentioned in a brief foreword. However, the bibliography at the end of this book gives an excellent overview.

Mara Selvini and her collaborators have made seminal contributions to our understanding of systems, and to problem-solving strategies and tactics made possible by this understanding. What was first briefly mentioned in her work *Paradox and Counterparadox* was greatly expanded in *The Magician Without Magic*, where —as far as I know, for the first time—it was shown that a large system may "need" the continued failure of one of its members in order to avoid the otherwise necessary changes of its structure.

These ideas now find an elaborate and elegant expression in the present volume. My best wishes go with this book.

Palo Alto   Paul Watzlawick

PREFACE

This book continues the story of the collaboration between myself (a psychiatrist and systemic family therapist) and a growing num ber of psychologists working in large organizations. It all began with an invitation to work with a group of educational psychologists, whom I had instructed in systems theory, at the Institute of Psychology in the Catholic University of Milan. I accepted, and while still pursuing research at the Center for Family Studies, I began work at the Institute of Psychology. The results of the family-research project were published in 1975 as *Paradosso e controparadosso (Paradox and Counterparadox)*. Our educational research group, which began work in 1972, published *Il mago smagato (The Magician Without Magic)* in 1976. We had arrived at three important conclusions:

- The educational psychologist, quietly and humbly, should inform the head of the school about the relational model he adopts in his work.

- He should apply for a definite period of observation.

- He should elaborate and submit a written program in which he specifies the work in detail, explaining, discussing, and, if necessary, reassessing and readjusting it, until his ideas are accepted as a contract by the head and by the teaching staff concerned.

But the work had proved unexpectedly thankless and the methodological problems enormous, so our educational psychologists called a halt to that particular research. However, I still wanted to continue an experiment that seemed closely connected with my work as a family therapist. Anyone who accepts Gregory Bateson's epistemology cannot help being fascinated by a conceptual model that connects things that used to be separate and offers a logical approach to anyone looking for implications and interconnections in an attempt to cross apparently insurmountable barriers.

In November 1976, I was offered a chance to continue my research on large systems. Again the request came from former students of mine, who differed from the last group in being professionally involved in a variety of organizations (such as business, hospitals, research centers, and schools). I accepted, hoping to profit from this variety. Our regular meetings, each about two hours, continued from November 1976 to January 1979—sixtynine in all. Thereafter, we met at irregular intervals to discuss the chapters each member was writing. As to method, we used the empirical approach of the previous group: each member would describe his relationship with "his" organization. Not unexpectedly, all the working members found themselves in serious difficulties. However, thanks to the experience gained with the previous group, we were soon able to identify the problems; most were the result of errors the psychologists had made on joining the organizations. These errors sometimes jeopardized their relationship with the organization to the point of paralysis.

During the first phase of our work, we tried to devise strategies to change such dysfunctional relationships. We succeeded in just one case, described in Chapter 3, and then only because the head of the organization was replaced, allowing a new approach that avoided the old mistakes. In another case, we made an important mistake: We adopted a medical model to the point of considering the company in question "sick" and searching for an appropriate "cure" for it.

However, despite our errors, even the first phase proved fruitful. Analyzing the concrete situations of our group members brought out an important fact: different organizations will, in certain circumstances, produce identical processes. It also became clear how the interaction between the psychologists and such organizational processes was responsible for many situations in which the psychologists' hands were tied. We were delighted with this discovery because we could derive a constant advantage from it: the psychologists involved thus discovered their true function in the organization. This helped them to avoid mistakes, and also to grasp the type of game being played in the organization and to take appropriate steps. These steps evolved into the concrete strategies and tactics set out in this book for the purpose of helping psychologists—and anyone else working in large organizations—not only to survive but also to create good working conditions.

Contrary to the usual prejudice of our culture, which overestimates the importance of verbal communication, our strategies are based essentially on nonverbal communication. For example, our school psychologist used certain tactics for conveying messages that, stated verbally, would have been offensive: he handed the mayor's letter of introduction to the head of the school district (instead of stating blatantly, "I'm not answerable to you but to the city . . ."); he installed a mailbox for use by anyone wanting to meet with him (not saying "I'm not the sort of person you stop in corridors"). In my opinion, any psychologist's success in constructively influencing an organization depends on his ability to communicate in this implicit fashion.

I am convinced that this book will prove useful not only to psychologists but to anyone working in organizations. As a private family therapist, I think without envy of those of my colleagues, also family therapists, who work in organizations (hospitals, local health centers). They are often in the impossible situation of having to play two simultaneous games: the family game and the organization game. If they lack the tools to decipher the organization game *first of all,* and thus fail to act in a constructive way, they may well find that their family work suffers as a result.

For my part, I am becoming more and more convinced of the value of pursuing both lines of research simultaneously. But despite the usefulness of a common conceptual model, the differences in the methods of research used in family therapy and in the study of large organizations are becoming increasingly plain. Still, I do not yet feel confident enough to venture a commentary on these differences. As Edgar Morin (1980)* has put it so shrewdly, "the method emerges from the research." Originally, he points out, the word *method* meant *path;* it is only in traveling that the path is found, and only in the course of research that the right method appears.

In my view, the very fact that the two types of related research have to follow two different paths, and hence to embrace two different methods, not only helps them complement and enrich each other but can, in the long run, prove highly creative. Gregory Bateson must have been thinking of much the same thing when he wrote in praise of the method of double or multiple comparison. "Consider," he says, "the case of binocular vision. I compared what could be seen with one eye with what could be seen with two eyes, and noted that in this comparison the two-eyed method of seeing disclosed an extra dimension called *depth*. But the two-eyed way of seeing is itself an act of comparison."[1]

Bateson encourages my hope that the confrontation of the two methods of research—into families and large systems—may one day reveal, quite spontaneously, that little extra: a third dimension.

Milan   Mara Selvini Palazzoli

---

*Works cited only by author or author and date are listed in the Bibliography, and numbered references are to the Notes section, both at the end of the book.

CONCRETE EXPERIENCES

A PSYCHOLOGIST IN INDUSTRY

The psychologist described here had been working in the company under discussion for about two years before he joined our research team. As a result, his situation in the company, by all accounts, could no longer be changed. Moreover, even before his appointment, he had been friendly with one of the two owners. Our account of the workings of the company reconstructs the interventions our team suggested to the psychologist. These were proposed for two main reasons. The first was to provoke responses likely to yield information that otherwise might not be forthcoming. The second, by contrast, was the result of the group's exasperation when it became clear that it could not influence the repetitive game of the partners. Deciding that the company was "sick" and in need of "therapy," the group proposed its interventions.

The end of the affair—the parting of the ways of the two owners (possibly influenced by the work of the psychologist)—seemed to confirm a repeated observation: the rules of some games in large systems may suddenly change if they begin to threaten the main players.

THE COMPANY

The company involved was a group of several factories run along strict lines by two owners who shared the top managerial functions. The president held 70 percent of the company's stock, and the vice-president 30 percent, but as Figure 1 shows, the two were on the same hierarchic level, despite their disproportionate shares in the company and their dissimilar responsibilities. The two men shared control of planning, administrative policy, research, special projects, and legal services. The president controlled financial, managerial, and personnel policies; the vice-president controlled manufacturing and sales—but there were no formal channels of communication and oversight between the two men. This anomaly was at the heart of a great many of the phenomena we observed.

THE PSYCHOLOGIST JOINS THE COMPANY

The way the president chose and appointed the psychologist reflected the repetitive game typical of the two owners (a game not identified by the research group until much later).

It should be noted that the psychologist had known the vice-president socially for quite some time, though the actual interview and appointment were arranged by the president. Presumably both partners were bound to agree on the choice of a professional who, being in their own social circle, would be least likely to enter into dangerous alliances with staff members.

The psychologist, although aware of the difficulties that might arise from his ambiguous relationship with the president and the vice-president, gladly accepted the job. Not only was the salary well above the average, but he also hoped that his friendship with the vice-president would give him greater leeway and influence in the organization as a whole. Finally, the opportunity to observe a large system from the inside was likely to yield fresh material for a paper he was writing.

The psychologist first met the president of the company in a nonprofessional context: an art exhibit. The president said that his partner had talked about him, and that he was very keen to see psychological methods applied to certain chronic problems in his

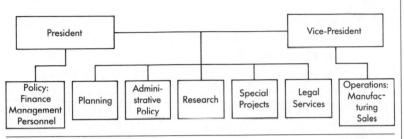

FIGURE 1.

company. He invited the psychologist to come to the office to discuss the possibility of a full-time job as an industrial psychologist.

At that meeting, the president gave the psychologist his views about the conflicts that were rife in the company, particularly in the departments of planning and management—conflicts that, he said, had spread to the rest of the company (to both his and his partner's departments). These conflicts had not only undermined the efficiency of the staff but also led to a high staff turnover. The president believed that these conflicts were closely connected with the personal history of those involved in them.

The main causes, he went on to say, were envy, rivalry, unsatisfied ambition, and such factors as ulcers and "bad family relations." "These are the people you'll be dealing with," he concluded.

The psychologist refused to accept that interpretation. He explained that he could not hope to resolve any conflicts if he confined his attention to staff dissatisfaction or strain. In his view, the organizational context in which these problems had developed would also have to be considered. He proposed a kind of contract: he would study the situation and conflicts in meetings with the senior staff of the various departments. He would report his findings to the partners at regular intervals, and propose appropriate remedies.

Unexpectedly, the president readily accepted this proposal. Indeed, he encouraged the psychologist to look into all the conflicts that were impeding the company's progress, and urged him to spare no one, and to "pay particular attention to those individuals who undermine company morale."

The psychologist, anxious to define his relationship with the various hierarchic levels, insisted on being formally presented to the vice-president, the personnel director, the departmental managers, and everyone else with whom he would have to work. Unfortunately, however, he had to resign himself to the president's decision to present him only to the vice-president, as "a formal and final seal on your appointment."

On that occasion, the vice-president proved surprisingly cool. His manner was the very opposite of the president's—in a tone ranging from irony to derision, he voiced his skepticism about psychology and psychologists. He added that psychologists had no function in industry: "When an employee has difficulties, it's easier to replace him than to make him adapt." In his opinion, psychological problems affected only "mediocre people who were too ambitious, and therefore quite useless to the company."

Though amazed, the psychologist soberly pointed out that a frustrated and maladjusted staff can cause not only a disagreeable atmosphere but also actual financial loss. The vice-president retorted that the company's earnings were too high for such losses to matter. All in all, he felt, hiring a psychologist was an utter waste of time. It was just another one of the president's whims—meant solely to show the world that he ran a model enterprise, and "nowadays no company can call itself a model enterprise unless it bends over backwards to pamper the staff." But since the psychologist's appointment was a *fait accompli,* he wanted to make it perfectly clear that any problems there might be were in departments under the president's control, certainly not in his own. He ran his own departments with purpose and authority, unlike his partner, who did nothing but confuse his staff. Disagreeable though that was, it in no way affected the vice-president's staff. With these words, the vice-president, pleading urgent business, ended his meeting with the psychologist.

Observations on how the psychologist was hired

If we examine the hiring of the psychologist, paying due attention to his own motives in accepting the provisos of his contract, we discover that his communications with the president and with the vice-president occurred at three distinct levels: explicit, implicit and secret.

- *The president's explicit request* was for the psychologist to help resolve conflicts in the company, which were due to the personal difficulties of certain employees. On the surface, the president offered the psychologist an *alliance for* ensuring the well-being of his staff, so as to improve company efficiency.

- *The president's implicit request* to the psychologist was that he not question the president's way of running the company, and that he pay particular attention to "those individuals" who undermine company morale. In practice, he offered the psychologist a *coalition against* anyone in the company trying to undermine his authority.

- *The president's secret agenda* was an attempt to gain control, through the psychologist, of the whole company, including manufacturing and sales. This explains his insistence that the psychologist look into all conflicts plaguing the company, even those in the sector run by the vice-president. Thus, it is easy to see why he was so quick to agree to the kind of contract proposed by the psychologist.

- *The vice-president* made no *explicit request.* The psychologist, he said, was of no practical use to the company. He nevertheless agreed that it was the "thing to do these days" to have a staff psychologist, and finally admitted the existence of conflicts in the president's sector. In practice, he granted the psychologist a mandate to deal with that sector.

- *The vice-president's implicit request* to the psychologist was that he must be left to run his own sector without interference.

- *The vice-president's secret agenda* was to prove himself superior to his partner and to show that his authority derived from his greater technical competence and more commanding personality.

- *The psychologist's explicit message* was that he wanted his analysis of company conflicts to involve the various subsystems affected by them. He would supply the partners with information based on his analysis of the relationship between the various department heads.

- *The psychologist's implicit message* was that he would not involve the partners themselves in his study, nor try to clarify the effects of the partners' behavior on the staff.

- *The psychologist's secret agenda* was to make a full systems analysis of the company.

Having reached a preliminary agreement with the partners, the psychologist went on to define his methods. To begin with, he would look into the problems that emerged during individual discussions with various employees. His written reports would then inform the partners about relational difficulties in the company. Finally, if the partners wished, he would discuss with them how to achieve the improvements. Beyond this work, which would take about half his working time, he would set aside a number of hours for interviews of prospective employees, and for individual meetings requested by staff members.

The psychologist sets to work

The psychologist began his work by arranging interviews with those employees who welcomed his presence. In his first report to the president, he presented some of his observations.

The president responded by saying that he had read the psychologist's reports attentively and appreciated his excellent work. But he never commented on the contents; he met the psychologist's specific findings with silence.

The vice-president let the psychologist know that he never read his reports and asked him "to put a stop to them very soon." Because no time limit had been set on the psychologist's investigation, this message was tantamount to a complete rejection of his work.

The most significant aspects of the developments so far are easily summed up:

- Although it was the vice-president who had known the psychologist socially and had suggested to the president that he be hired, it was the president who appointed him and showed interest in his professional skill.

- Once the psychologist was hired, the vice-president adopted an attitude of permanent rejection, while the president demonstrated his esteem, encouraging the study and promising full support.

The psychologist was understandably confused. Only later did he learn that the two heads of the company had behaved the same way whenever a consultant or a senior staff member was hired: the new person was invariably welcomed by the president and ignored by the vice-president. This repetitive pattern was a crucial discovery for our research group. Without realizing it, the psychologist was in the same situation as the staff members he was expected to help: supported by the president and spurned by the vice-president. In fact, however, the president's support was a sham: he expressed thanks and formal approval, but beyond that he met the psychologist's messages with complete silence. His formal support thus concealed an essential rejection.

THE FIRST "PATIENT": THE CHEMIST

The first staff member to ask for a meeting was a chemist. He was deeply dissatisfied with his work, and worried about its repercussions on his private life and mental health. He complained that he was unable to exercise his professional skills because his superiors and his colleagues had set up an insurmountable wall of hostility.

During two meetings with the psychologist, the chemist listed the events that had led to the present impasse. A year earlier, the president had hired him to plan the process of buying raw materials. He was told that he would be directly responsible to the vice-president, who was in charge of his department. From the first day, however, he realized that the vice-president neither appreciated his professional standing nor recognized the job for which he had been hired. In fact, each time he asked for information, he was obstructed in so many ways that he felt completely hamstrung. Worse still, the vice-president did not even return his greeting when they happened to pass each other.

From his brief case history, we gathered that the man we called our first "patient" had, in his previous job, shown a dogged determination to be a reformer, against the advice of his superiors.

As a result, he had lost a very good post a few years earlier. Nonetheless, even in his present plight, he persisted in suggesting changes in any purchasing arrangements proposed by the vice-president or his colleagues, with the result that he had become completely isolated.

After two meetings, the chemist asked the psychologist to suggest ways of clearing the air.

The psychologist's reactions to the request were complex. He wished to help the man who had appealed to him, and he also hoped to gather information about the way the company really worked and thus to help change things for the better. He proposed to intervene on two levels:

- He would deal with the explicit needs of the employee—his anxieties and the tensions that rendered his professional position intolerable.

- He wanted to intervene in the company system, by treating the "patient" as a "symptom."

In short, he was treating the chemist as a professional client even while considering the "sick system" as his real subject.

The patient had become a means for the psychologist to gather information about relations and methods of communication in the company, with a view to overhauling the whole system. That objective, however, was unrealistic, since the partners had made it clear that the psychologist was expected only to deal with restless employees; moreover, he had implied when negotiating his contract that he would not extend his investigations to the workings of the partners.

However, the information the psychologist gathered on the chemist's problems—particularly the way he was appointed—threw light on the modes of interaction used at the top. It seems the chemist, then in a senior post in another company, had heard from a friend that this company was looking for an expert to reform the purchasing department. Excited by this prospect, he asked his friend to recommend him for the job. The friend spoke to the president, who immediately summoned the chemist for a preliminary interview. At the end of their meeting, the president said he was ready to put him in charge of modernizing purchasing procedures. He then offered a most generous salary and asked him to present himself to the vice-president to discuss his employment. The chemist called on the vice-president, but had hardly entered his office when the president burst in and peremptorily confirmed the chemist's appointment.

The chemist, assuming that he had a relatively free hand and was responsible to the partners alone, soon discovered that he was expected to take orders from the head of the purchasing department, who took his orders from the vice-president! In fact it was not until after he had started work that the president showed him his precise place in the company chain of command.

What amazed our chemist was not so much the equivocation and intrigue surrounding these early contacts as the president's refusal to present him to the manager of the purchasing department, on the pretext that the manager was "a difficult customer whom it is best not to antagonize." The chemist was then introduced to the personnel director, who was to formalize his appointment.

The chemist was amazed. And the manager of the purchasing department was absolutely indignant. He had been told nothing about the new appointment. Not surprisingly, his relationship with the chemist was ruined from the outset, the manager completely ignoring a man about whose appointment he had never been consulted.

The chemist, for his part, felt that his qualifications entitled him to bypass his direct superior, and began to devise a purchasing plan of his own. This elicited a *symmetrical* reaction (that is, a response in kind) from the manager, who began to treat the chemist with even greater disdain. In particular, he refused to look at the chemist's plan, ignored his requests for information, and refused to speak to him on the telephone or in his office.

The result was a negative spiral of symmetrical interactions. The chemist appealed to the president for help in getting the information he needed. In reply, the president told him again that the manager was a difficult customer who had to be treated with a great deal of tact. At the same time the president encouraged him to persevere and to continue his good work.

The chemist then made a fresh attempt to make peace with the manager, but the latter clearly would not relent unless the chemist acknowledged his authority. At this point, the chemist told the president he was prepared to take orders from the manager and cease being a "reformer." The president, however, ordered him to do nothing of the kind, and reminded him why he was hired.

So the chemist tried once again to get the information he needed from the manager, but again came up against a stone wall. He asked the president once more to intervene. He got no reply. His frustration at being unable to change the situation in any way had by now brought him to the verge of a nervous breakdown.

One afternoon after work, the chemist had a serious car accident, due largely to his extreme nervousness. He was told that his injuries would keep him in the hospital for at least six months.

As soon as the president heard about the crash, he appointed the chemist to the permanent staff, though his probationary period was not yet over; he reassured him that his job was safe and he could count on the company's full support. Moreover, after he left the hospital, he would have a car and chauffeur until he was once more able to drive himself.

Let us now look at the various levels of communication between the president and the chemist.

- *The president's explicit request to the chemist* was that he modernize the purchasing methods—a request for an open *alliance for* increasing company profits.

- *The president's implicit request to the chemist* was that he exercise control over the purchasing department by means of a buying plan that bypassed the department—a request for a *coalition against* those in charge of the department.

- *The president's secret agenda* was to gain control over the manufacturing sector, for which his partner bore sole responsibility.

- *The chemist's explicit request* was for a prominent position in which he could prove his ability—in other words, an *alliance* with the president *for* reforming an entire sector of the enterprise.

- *The chemist's implicit request* was to be answerable exclusively to the president and to share his powers—in effect, to form a *coalition against* the chemist's immediate superior.

- *The chemist's secret agenda* was to fulfill ambitions that had been thwarted in his last job.

Clearly the chemist's appointment reflected a perverse coalition, uniting two men on different hierarchic levels (the president and the chemist) against a third (the vice-president), of a higher level than the chemist.

Officially, this coalition was denied through a series of nonverbal communications. The president, for instance, did not present the chemist to the manager of the purchasing department, which suggested that he had no wish to interfere in his partner's area. Still, he had personally hired a professional expressly to modernize a department in that area. As a result, the chemist received contradictory messages from the president: assigning a car and driver to him seemed to indicate a privileged relationship with the president; yet sending him to the personnel department when he was hired instead of presenting him in person to his superior seemed to have stamped him as an ordinary employee. Similarly, the president's insistence on the chemist's reforming the purchasing methods did not jibe with his tacit refusal to intervene on the chemist's behalf. In other words, while the coalition was affirmed at certain levels of communication, it was denied at others.

So far we have looked at communications between the president and the chemist as if they involved only the two of them. But the reality was quite different. In fact, the discordant messages cease to be confusing as soon as we extend our analysis to include the other true protagonist, the vice-president. It then becomes clear that *what the chemist interprets as a snub from the president is, in fact, a message of nonbelligerence from the president to his partner:* "You see that I have not allied myself with him, that I treat him just like any other employee." Hence our "patient" emerges as a pawn in the president's conflict with his partner—a willing pawn because of his consuming ambition.

This leads us to reflect on the complexity of communication in organizations, and on their consequences. Often an individual in an organization thinks all the rejections that reach him are addressed exclusively to him. If so, these messages may wound him deeply, undermining both his professional performance and his mental balance. This often happens when a person (or group) is a pawn in a conflict between two other parties and is unaware of the fact.

Every relational context (a group, a company, a family) potentially involves more than two-way communication, because any one message can have several addressees. In the case of our chemist, what struck him as a rejection was meant as a message of reassurance to the vice-president (and his subordinates). If we use a wider —say a triadic—approach, we shall find that such rejections (and even such stronger communications as repudiation) do not fit the pattern described by Laing (1961), by Laing, Phillipson, and Lee (1966), and by Watzlawick *et al.* (1967). In the wider perspective, the message "You are not there, you have no part in any relationship with me" is addressed not to just one person but, through him, to others, the sender being unwilling or unable to send that message directly.

In this perspective, even repudiation ceases to be gratuitously cruel, as it invariably is in a dyadic perspective (see Laing, 1961). Instead it reflects complex relationships that have gradually developed into conflictual systems tempered by the imperative of avoiding open conflicts.

All messages of confirmation, rejection, and repudiation should therefore be considered in the framework of wider communications. In a company, this wider context is obvious: one person's role clearly impinges on everyone else's. Thus, messages of confirmation or repudiation, though ostensibly addressed to a person, are more generally addressed to his role in the organization. Therefore the analysis of such communications must embrace levels of complexity that are hard to grasp, particularly by the people involved. We shall consider this aspect at greater length in the last chapter.

THE SECOND "PATIENT": THE ENGINEER

The second "patient" was an engineer in charge of business with developing countries. He was confused and worried about his position in the company. He had been put in charge of a recently formed subsidiary, whose purely financial objectives were to examine and propose possible investments in developing countries. It employed five senior managers lured away from good posts at other companies by high salaries. But, after a year of studying investment plans and making contacts abroad, the senior staff realized that investment prospects were negligible, because the company did not have enough capital for the ambitious plans first broached. The managers felt disappointed and humiliated. Not only had their efforts come to naught, but the partners offered no adequate explanation. Worse, the partners didn't bother to inform them about future objectives—so all they could do was continue to make contacts and propose fresh initiatives, all futile, with no guidance about future work. The vice-president, moreover, openly disapproved of the subsidiary and clearly believed it had no chance of finding useful investments. The position of those in the subsidiary thus became highly equivocal. Though they were paid generous salaries, they were constantly frustrated. Meanwhile, the partners were inconsistent: while the president continually called for studies and contacts, the vice-president refused to take any interest in their "futile projects." This went on for a whole year; finally people started resigning. At this point the engineer approached the psychologist, as an expert in communication, for help in clarifying the situation—at least on a personal level.

The psychologist tried to analyze the partners' possible motives:

- *The partners' explicit request:* The experts hired to run the new subsidiary must concern themselves with creating and planning new investments. These would reflect the company's general policy of expanding into developing countries.

- *The partners' implicit request:* Though the experts shall draw up projects, they must not concern themselves with their implementation, which is the partners' business. The experts' salaries ought to give them all the satisfaction they need.

- *The partners' secret agenda:* The company, instead of investing its own capital in developing countries, would try to persuade these countries to invest their own capital in expansion programs. (This last point emerged from careful study of company behavior and correspondence.)

The engineer agreed with the psychologist's analysis, and granted that, in principle, the objectives of the company should take precedence over those of the individuals it employs. Nevertheless, he decided to resign because he found the situation too frustrating. He asked, however, that the psychologist advise him how to resign in the most dignified way. He feared that, once in the president's office, he might lose his self-control, but he wanted to avoid a scene, since he had been offered a post in an associated company.

The engineer's objectives can be summed up as follows:

- *Explicit request:* "Help me resign with dignity." This request seemed bizarre, since the engineer was used to handling high-level social contacts. But significantly, it illustrated the enormous emotional tension the engineer and his colleagues were under in their jobs.

- *Implicit request:* "Help me not to be swamped by my emotions" (a therapeutic request).

- *Secret agenda:* "Help me show the president that I have not failed, that I am more far-sighted than he thinks." The engineer wanted to leave a good impression on the president, who could be useful in his future career.

The psychologist agreed to help the engineer. He also secretly decided to use the resignation to send a message to the partners strong enough to make them change course. He enlisted the help of our research group, to which he had recently explained his own position in the company. After due reflection, the group suggested that the engineer should characterize the president's past attitude very positively when submitting his resignation. Such a positive connotation not only would help the engineer resign with dignity, but, they hoped, it might also bring the president to his senses by startling him with an entirely unexpected approach.

The group suggested that the engineer address the president roughly as follows:

"As soon as I joined your company, I realized that it deserved my total commitment. You assembled a team of men whose brilliant professional careers should have guaranteed success. However, for reasons quite beyond me, we seem to have created a structure which, far from helping to implement the company's objectives, has put obstacles in its path. And yet you have continued to do your best to ensure that no one felt neglected. It is quite obvious that the creation of new investment projects calls for the constant modification of plans, and that senior staff cannot expect to be issued guidelines whose sole purpose it is to bolster their egos.

"I realize that this situation is bound to worry you. All of us appreciate how hard you have tried to support the emotional stability of your staff by involving them in projects that unfortunately cannot be implemented just now. I also realize that the best we managers can do for the company is to be patient, to apply ourselves to the task at hand, and not to worry about the final results. Though we cannot expect quick professional credit, we must nevertheless continue to create plans and programs.

"I realize all that; if I hand in my resignation anyway, it is because of my own impatient desire for quick results. Knowing my own shortcomings, I have decided to leave this company, which needs more patient and persistent men. Once the company is rid of individuals with too-rigid expectations, no doubt the company will be able to fulfill its objectives."

Afterward, the engineer reported on his meeting with the president:

The president, having listened to the engineer, did his utmost to give a negative connotation to the way the company was being run and to his own style of leadership. It would have been much easier for him to react to outright criticism than to such an ambiguous communication. The engineer, carefully instructed by the psychologist on how to counter this maneuver, did not fall into the president's trap but kept criticizing his own moral failure to cope with a situation that was undoubtedly important, even if not immediately satisfying.

The object of the exercise was to reveal the behavior of the partners and the obscure reasons for their creating the new subsidiary. The result was a battle of wits between the engineer and the president, who eventually supplied the information he had always withheld, hoping to take the engineer by surprise and trick him into criticizing the company's methods.

The meeting lasted three hours, each man sticking to his guns. Toward the end, the president appeared depressed, and began to accuse himself of incompetence and failure to provide leadership. The meeting, and the engineer's employment, ended on that note.

The psychologist reported the episode to the research group. The president's depressive reaction had satisfied both our second "patient," who could leave the company "with dignity" (and with the apologies of the president), and the research group, who felt the intervention had succeeded in causing a marked change in the president's behavior.

But that view had to be revised when the psychologist learned about the president's actions after the meeting.

One of the vice-president's men—who, like his chief, had been opposed to the formation of the subsidiary—told anyone who would listen that he had just been in the vice-president's office when the president burst in. With an air of triumph, he had recounted his turbulent meeting with the engineer, who had handed in his resignation for purely careerist motives. That meeting, according to the president, had revealed the extreme importance of the subsidiary and convinced him that it was certainly worth persevering with it. The vice-president's sole response was to continue signing his correspondence in total silence.

It thus appears that after the depression the engineer observed, the president had had a complete change of heart. The "therapeutic" effect of the research group's maneuver thus seemed highly questionable.

The president's depressive reaction was accordingly reassessed as a countermaneuver designed to elicit sympathy and respect from the engineer.

The group concluded that the game at the top (between the president and the vice-president) took precedence over all other interactions, including the one between the president and the engineer.

At this point, let us see how the company's organizational chart looks when modified in the light of our findings.

THE COMPANY ORGANIZATION: AN ANALYSIS OF PARADOXES

As the reader will gather from Figure 2, the president and vice-president were on the same hierarchic level, while fulfilling different functions and holding unequal shares of the company's stock. They jointly supervised planning, administrative policy, research,

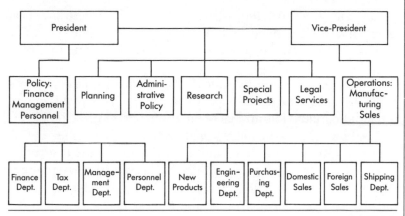

FIGURE 2.

special projects, and legal services. The president controlled economic and financial policy, management, and personnel; the vice-president controlled manufacturing and sales.

The president's sector included finance, taxes, management, and personnel; the other sector, run by the vice-president, comprised domestic and foreign sales, manufacturing policy, purchasing, shipping, and new products.

Oddly enough, the official company organizational chart bore the following legend: "The levels shown on this chart do not necessarily reflect actual functions."

Because of this loose arrangement, it was always possible to bypass the normal chain of command, and this loophole caused major conflicts. Every manager felt entitled to appeal directly to either partner, thus snubbing his immediate superiors. Also, the normal flow of information was often short-circuited.

Moreover, if financial, managerial, and personnel policy are on the same level as manufacturing and sales policy, the realities of business organization are ignored, and all lines of communication are crossed and disrupted. Companies normally devise medium- and long-term strategies on which to base their commercial policy. The specific concern of financial and management policy is to make the best possible long-term use of the company's capital and labor resources, while manufacturing and sales are concerned with the more immediate problems of what to produce, when, and at what price. It follows that the two types of policy cannot be placed on the same footing without disrupting the chain of command.

In our case, we must wonder if the sole aim of the company's hierarchic arragement was not to make the two partners feel equally important. The arrangement was bound to cause problems.

Ultimately, the financial-policy sector was given only routine tasks to do. It ceased to have any real influence on the company's economic and financial policy, which had become the sole prerogative of the president. The vice-president, being jointly responsible for running the company, ought also to have had some say in the company's economic and financial policy. On the other hand, he controlled manufacturing totally.

The structure obviously stood in the way of joint control of the two sectors. The president could not control his partner's sector because the latter, as his equal, could tell him to mind his own business. Nor could the vice-president help frame economic and financial policy. In the end, that didn't really bother the vice-president, since he could always influence how it was carried out —as head of operations, he could override the strategies chosen by the president. The usual hierarchic gap between the policy-making and operational sectors was thus reversed in favor of the latter.

The reader can now appreciate the significance of the disclaimer on the official chart, and see why the president felt so great a need to display control over the vice-president. The disclaimer turned the chart into a paradoxical statement asserting on one level (formal, hierarchical) what it denied on another (functional). This paradox echoed the situation at the top: the president and vice-president were ostensibly equal, when in fact each was desperately trying to gain more power than the other.

THE THIRD "PATIENT": THE NEW MANAGER

It should now be clear that the interactions of the two partners had the practical effect of paralyzing all initiatives from senior managers. During the two years the psychologist had been on the staff, the company had witnessed many bitter conflicts, mainly involving the president's policy-making team. Unlike the operational sector, where the staff seemed adequately motivated, capable, and united, the policy team had a 55 percent turnover—a very high rate, usually a sign of growing discontent. New young managers found working conditions intolerable and rapidly lost interest, so most resigned. This left a team of old managers who had watched the company grow and hence felt emotionally involved; in any case, most were too old to find rewarding alternatives. The younger men usually said they were resigning because job satisfaction was low in the company; there was a sense of confinement, of being manipulated by the partners, whose aims seemed obscure.

Discontent reached such levels that the policy team indulged in a symmetrical escalation of hostility, expressed in exaggeratedly competitive behavior.[1]

The psychologist, after listening to several staff members, reported their complaints to the partners. He wrote that the trouble could be attributed to a number of factors. First, the complaints reflected the lack of communication, either horizontal or vertical. The staff tended not to exchange information between departments for fear of having it used against them. The upshot was that each department had an inflated view of its own importance, coupled with suspicion of all others, seen as potential enemies. Worse still, the flow of information between the president and his senior staff was cut, which confused them further and increased their sense of insecurity. They complained of having ill-defined responsibilities, of not knowing the precise limits of their authority. They also objected to the lack of coordination between the top echelon and the various department heads, which they felt impeded communication and decision-making.

The report was read by the president, who made some comments and thanked the psychologist for his excellent work, but did not offer to discuss possible changes.

The vice-president, for his part, showed no interest in the report and repeated his wish not to be bothered about what went on in the president's sector.

When the partners failed to propose any improvements in the situation, many of the managers resigned. Others tried to improve matters through minor changes in their own departments. One in particular hoped to involve the partners *in a process of change starting from the bottom.*

This man—we shall call him the "new manager" because he

had been appointed quite recently—tried to interest the partners in a project to create working groups, involving the heads of the various departments, that would function for limited periods on specific tasks. He felt this project would meet a double objective:

- It would improve working conditions by facilitating the flow of information between department heads.

- It would lay the foundations for a type of coordination that could be extended to the whole company, if the project's results were good.

As the reader will realize, this was an attempt to change the company's structure through work on a concrete project. The partners would be faced with data that would justify a change of organization—data derived from focusing attention on concrete tasks rather than on bad relationships. Having elaborated his project, the new manager asked the psychologist how to promote his idea without antagonizing his potential collaborators. Let us analyze his request:

- *Explicit request:* To enlist the psychologist's help in setting up working groups intended to smooth the flow of information between departments and to introduce an operational model of staff management focused on the task at hand and not on relationships.

- *Implicit request:* To support his implicit exclusion from the project of the most powerful departments, and his inclusion only of the managers who approved of his plan. In practice, he planned a coalition with his sympathizers against his opponents.

- *Secret agenda:* To use his project as a stepping-stone for his ambition to become general coordinator of the entire administrative sector.

The psychologist agreed, entering into an explicit alliance with the new manager to improve departmental operations and staff cohesion. Implicitly, he accepted a coalition against the partners, who seemed determined to keep absolute control over the company.

Meanwhile our research group, to which the psychologist reported his experiences, grew more curious and ambitious. While helping the new manager, the psychologist also hoped to use his project as a means to inject new information into the company's relational system and thus initiate a change. He proposed that the new manager send a series of memoranda to the partners—drawn up with the help of all the managers interested in the project.

The psychologist himself sent a report to the partners discussing the difficult situation of the various department heads. Their discontent and consequent loss of commitment, he pointed out, had led to a spate of errors that had harmed the company; a major problem was the fact that the department heads worked independently and lacked channels of communication. He also stressed that the managers would feel happier if, instead of bonuses and other material incentives, they got a measure of professional satisfaction from their work. In particular, he asked the partners to encourage group involvement, which would help senior managers to identify more closely with the company.

At the same time, the partners received a note from one manager saying that he was unable to do his work without the collaboration of a working group made up of members of the various departments. And last but not least, the new manager asked the partners to approve the creation of working groups centered on specific company objectives, and to put an end to the waste of time and the lack of communication implicit in the division of labor among isolated sectors.

Whereupon the partners thanked the psychologist and discussed his report of complaints by heads of departments, but were careful not to accept his proposal to change the situation—and completely ignored the other two reports.

Soon afterwards, those managers who had not been included in the new manager's project—and had guessed his hidden motives —protested to the partners and threatened to resign *en bloc* if his project were approved. The president reassured them—a move that caused the new manager to resign a few months later. His resignation, however, was rendered less unpleasant by the sympathy of the president, who declared that, because of the narrow-mindedness of the majority, he had been forced despite himself to turn his back on so fine a colleague.

This, then, is the account of the failure of the psychologist's (and the research group's) third attempt to change the rules of the game played at the top.

WHY THE MANAGEMENT DEPARTMENT DIDN'T WORK

A young manager who had been head of the management department for three years asked the psychologist for help. He explained that he had not yet been able to take control of his own problem-filled department. Previous managers who had tried to run it effectively had always failed, and had never enjoyed the support of the partners or of their colleagues. These obstacles still hindered not just the department's head, but its entire staff, who were always quarreling.

The atmosphere had lately grown less tense because the partners, alerted to the constant bickering, tried to resolve the problem by reducing the department to performing only routine tasks that called for no decisions.

The manager, an expert in industrial management, asked the psychologist if he wanted to collaborate on a study of the strange situation in the management department. He would look at the purely technical aspects, and the psychologist would deal with the prevailing relationships in the company.

The psychologist, disregarding the manager's implicit and secret motives, welcomed the invitation. So did the rest of our group—we felt that he might thus gain a clearer picture of the situation.

The collaboration did, in fact, isolate the essential factors responsible for the failure of all attempts by the management department to reorganize the company.

- The root of the trouble was clearly that, in the company's organization, the management department was not part of top management but was relegated to a subsidiary role. Instead of drawing up plans for the partners, it had been turned into a rubber stamp.

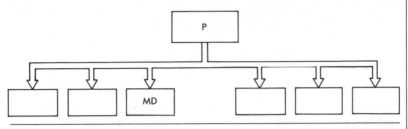

FIGURE 3.

- Another impediment was the absence of any mechanism for evaluating progress. If a management department is to improve the company's efficiency, it must constantly check on progress throughout the company. This is usually done by the department's head himself or by an inspector responsible to him. By contrast, in this company the partners alone considered themselves entitled to perform such general checks. Therefore the partners had effectively taken direct control over all the individual departments, as shown in Figure 3.

  Had these departments been linked along the normal lines, company resources would have been used more rationally—but that would have decentralized control (see Figure 4).

- Another obstacle to proper management was the impossibility of calling joint meetings with the partners and the heads of other departments to discuss company objectives. Clearly, the heads of the management, planning, and administrative policy departments, as senior managers, not only should be familiar with these objectives, but should also be able to examine them with the partners. In our case, the partners never consulted their managers on these matters and invariably opposed any of their proposals. In these circumstances it was never possible to use company resources optimally.

The division of power between the two chiefs—one controlling manufacturing and sales, and the other finance and administration—militated against common decisions for efficiency. The

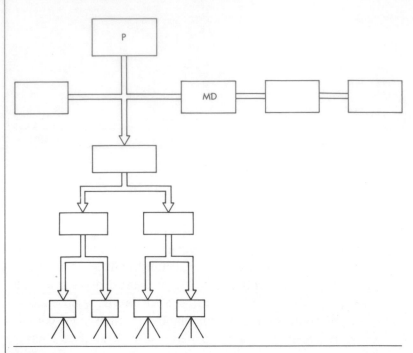

FIGURE 4.

analysis by the psychologist and the management department head highlighted the underlying reasons for the failure of every attempt to solve the company's internal problems by reorganization.

Now, while clearly defining the role of the management department would have increased the efficiency of the entire company, it would have robbed the partners of their arbitrary powers, since the department would, by definition, have assumed responsibility for many of the company's activities.

The analysis enabled the psychologist and our research group to clarify the particular conflict at the top of the company. The absurd structure of the company, relegating a top-level department to a subsidiary level under the direct control of the president, enabled him to dictate general policy at will and to ride roughshod over his managers. This evoked a symmetrical reaction from the vice-president, who frustrated every attempt by his partner to intervene in the sector under the vice-president's control. Reluctant to oppose the president's decisions overtly, he simply disparaged the president's managers, declaring them to be incompetent and uniting his own managers against them. As a result, the management department was completely isolated. Its sole job was to draw up lists of projects and allocations, to develop "procedures likely to facilitate communication," and to update the organizational chart—but certainly not to propose structural reforms.

DIAGRAMMING THE COMPANY'S EQUILIBRIUM

We found that the worst-functioning part of the company was the policy sector, directly controlled by the president. By contrast, the operations sector, under the vice-president, seemed stable, compact, and loyal to its head.

Viewing the company as a system, the subsystem *president + associates* seemed the least integrated, the most riddled with conflicts, and the least productive.

The question therefore arises whether the strict complementarity of the two apparently separate sectors—namely, the inefficient sector *(president + policy team),* and the super-efficient sector *(vice-president + operations team)*—was not, in fact, an arrangement that functioned to maintain repetitive patterns of behavior in the company game, with the practical result of blocking innovation and leaving total control in the hands of the two partners, who were apparently at loggerheads.[2]

This interpretation is diagrammed in Figure 5, showing that the president's behavior has three simultaneous objectives:

- To impress the outside world.

- To impress those working within the enterprise.

- To reach a concrete goal.

The president wanted to show the outside world that he headed a modern and efficient organization with a highly qualified staff. To the staff, he wanted to seem an audacious innovator. His concrete goal was to attract funds from both the public and the private sectors. In order to underline his innovative zeal, he appointed a string of experts on planning, industrial organization, and

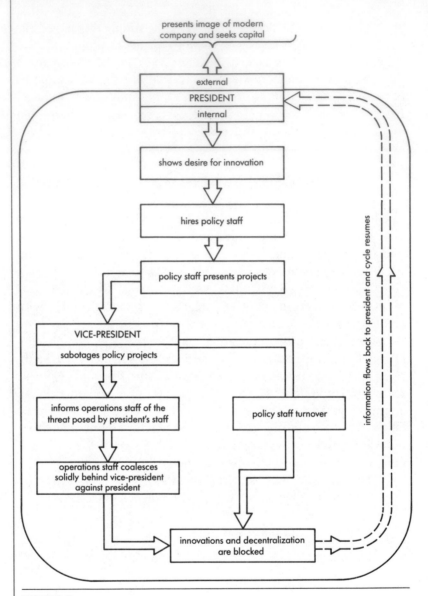

presents image of modern
company and seeks capital

external
PRESIDENT
internal

shows desire for innovation

hires policy staff

policy staff presents projects

VICE-PRESIDENT
sabotages policy projects

informs operations staff of the
threat posed by president's staff

policy staff turnover

operations staff coalesces
solidly behind vice-president
against president

information flows back to president and cycle resumes

innovations and decentralization
are blocked

FIGURE 5.

business administration, whom he asked for policy suggestions,
plans, and innovations.

The vice-president, for his part, had nothing but contempt for the president's staff, declaring them incapable of coming up with an effective policy. He accordingly rejected and blocked all projects submitted by the experts, thus hampering them professionally and provoking them to resign. At the same time, he harangued his own staff about how threatening these projects were. As a result, the employees in operations were united against the alleged enemy and solidly ranged behind their chief. In this way the operations sector, blocking all innovations, enabled the partners to maintain absolute control.

This game also entailed the fair distribution of "blame" between the two partners: the president was accused by the planners of inefficiency and inability to direct his own staff, while the vice-president was considered reactionary, deaf to the need for innovation. And it was precisely by thus sharing the "blame" that these two men were able to stay in control.

THE PSYCHOLOGIST CONFRONTS THE PARTNERS

We reached these conclusions during our first working year. But faced with the repetitive nature of events in the company and with our own inability to effect changes, the group began after a year to lose patience. Having diagnosed the root of the trouble, the members were not content to continue as mere observers.

In particular, it had become clear that the psychologist was in the same situation as other senior staff members—frustrated by the impossibility of doing anything valuable or satisfying.

As we will see, the group's sympathetic identification with the "unfortunate" staff reflected a symmetrical tendency *to redefine its relationship* with the partners *irrespective of the contractual terms* the psychologist had accepted.

Remember that the psychologist, when negotiating his contract, had implied that he would not extend his analysis to the leadership of the partners. Nevertheless, the group now decided to show them that the psychologist was not a helpless pawn, that he saw through their game. So they drew up a plan not unlike the game the psychologist had advised his second "patient"—the engineer—to play when he wished to resign "with dignity." The group

knew it was risking the psychologist's position, but he didn't mind
—he had taken about all he could from the partners.

The first thing was to choose the right moment. The group
agreed to wait until the psychologist was consulted about a fresh
crisis, which would call for a report. In his report, he would introduce a number of direct references to the partners' own behavior.
But how?

The group hit on the idea of a paradoxical commentary. The
psychologist would end his report by describing the roles played by
the president and the vice-president, giving both roles a positive
connotation and implying that they were indispensable to the
prestige and effective leadership of the company—something
like this:

"The frequent attempts by the staff to introduce innovations
and to propose changes are bound to have dangerous consequences
inasmuch as they undermine the authority of the partners. However, it is equally important for the partners to present, particularly
to the outside world, the image of a modern, dynamic company
pioneering new techniques and developments. Consequently, the
president's policy of engaging highly qualified managers versed in
the latest techniques, and that of the vice-president of stifling all
projects likely to endanger the stability of the company, not only
are highly effective but fulfill two needs. Caution towards innovative projects helps to reassure the operations sector (whose stability
is threatened) and to range it solidly behind its chief. Such complementary policies are also essential for maintaining control without
eliciting hostility from the staff, especially from those newly appointed managers who are pressing for innovations. In spite of the
vice-president's disapproval, they know that they can count on the
full support of the president.

"There are some drawbacks, of course: The vice-president is
accused of conservatism and authoritarianism, and the president of
incompetence and poor leadership. But proper control of the entire
company must take precedence over such secondary objectives as
staff satisfaction, and it justifies the large staff turnover."

The group assumed that this description of the homeostatic
game of the system might help the psychologist to induce a change
at the top.

When the staff returned from summer vacation, the psychologist was consulted about a serious conflict between the senior staff

of the administrative policy department and their immediate superior. For quite some time the staff had been disagreeing with the methods he used and had repeatedly proposed alternatives, which he systematically rejected. At long last they responded with what can only be called a mutiny: they ceased to do any work and refused to take orders from a man they considered technically incompetent and incapable of solving the department's problems.

The conflict was brought before the partners by both parties. The president listened to the staff's plea for a director whose leadership was more in keeping with the company's resources, but refused to side with them. Instead he bolstered the authority of their chief by endorsing the very decisions to which the staff objected.

At this point the dissidents turned to the psychologist and asked him to act as mediator. The psychologist listened to their complaints and to the alternative policies they proposed. He then inquired in other departments about the substance of their complaints and discovered that most senior staff agreed with them. Many, in fact, had already resigned from the company.

The psychologist then decided that the time had come to submit the kind of report our research group had worked out. To his surprise, this time he received no acknowledgment, not even a formal one.

THE RESULTS

The six weeks after the psychologist submitted his report were eventful

At first the psychologist received no indication whatsoever about the impact of his report. His relations with the president and vice-president were confined to formal courtesies during chance encounters. No changes were made in the way the company was run.

Then, quite suddenly, a series of events exploded, indicating a change in the partners' attitude. Even so, the psychologist was a passive spectator. The only word he got was a brief, cryptic message from the president. But let us set out the sequence of events:

■ The managers who had resigned following their clash with their chief were rehired on new terms. They were given executive posts in the administrative policy department, which no longer answered to the president, but now solely to the vice-president. Their former head was transferred to data processing and information. At this point the vice-president ran into the psychologist and said to him in what seemed a sardonic tone, "You won. I hope you're satisfied now." This unexpected message stupefied the psychologist. What did the vice-president mean? Had he read the psychologist's report and acted accordingly? In fact there seemed to have been something of a palace revolution, culminating in the ascendancy of the vice-president.

■ A conflict between the two chiefs of the personnel department, which had been raging for years, was suddenly resolved. These two men had suffered from a lack of definition in their respective functions. The first, appointed by the vice-president when the company was founded, had been joined, about two years before the events now described, by the second, a younger man who was selected by the psychologist at the behest of the president—ostensibly to cope with the much larger staff. The younger man refused to play second fiddle to the older, who frustrated every attempt to encroach upon his territory. The young chief repeatedly appealed to the president to define their respective spheres of authority, but always in vain. The solution of the conflict came quite unexpectedly and without discussion. The partners transferred the older chief to staff management of one of the factories, and handed over the management of the rest to the younger man.

This time, victory seemed to have gone to the president ("A morsel for one does harm to none," as the Italian proverb has it).

■ The third change was officially announced—a restructuring of the entire company. The president and vice-president would part company, and each would be running a separate enterprise. They had recently acquired another company in the same line of business, which would be directed by the vice-president, while the president would become the sole head of the mother company.

Once this decision had been made, things began to happen rapidly. All heads of department were promoted. The staff of the operations sector, always squarely behind the vice-president, could now work without any tensions. The internal situation of the mother company seemed to have recovered its balance, and all the old conflicts seemed to have been resolved—though some discontent could be detected among those who had not been promoted.

The president himself began to act differently. He no longer worked flat-out as he had done before, but took weekends and other periods off from work. No doubt he was no longer so desperate to present the image of a model enterprise to the outside world, since acquiring the new company assured him a near-monopoly in his field.

With peace established, the psychologist—who had remained with the president—found himself relegated to the job of selecting new staff. There was no longer any talk of teams of high-level consultants; all that was required now was to plan the routine work in an "organic" and functional way. As soon as the company had filled the remaining managerial posts, the psychologist was no longer needed. He was soon asked to leave the company.

REFLECTIONS AFTER THE EVENT

During the next year, our group had many occasions to reflect on this case. In particular we were unable to define the precise role of the psychologist; we could only speculate about it. Our chief hypothesis was that, by his general behavior and not merely by his final report, he had accelerated a process that began well before his appointment. The partners would, in any case, have had to reconsider their policies, once the perennial conflicts had spilled over into an important sector of the managerial team. Unfortunately, neither the psychologist nor the research group had the information needed to retrace the course of this process.

What had really happened to the pair at the top? How real was their eventual separation? The team could state categorically only that these two men still headed an industrial complex that dominated its field.

The most likely explanation, we thought, was that the resolution of the events sprang from a concerted strategy designed to provide a dignified way out of a situation that had become intolerable. In any case, once the separation had been announced, the fate of the psychologist in the company was settled, as was that of those specialists whose sole purpose had been to project an image that was no longer needed.

We also wondered if the position of the psychologist would have been different had he enjoyed the support of our research group from the start. Probably not: He would not have been offered full-time employment by these partners on any conditions but these. Had he been called in as an outside consultant to deal with a specific crisis, his role might have been quite different.[3] However, these reflections were mere speculation, and all the group could do was hope that more facts would appear in due course.

A PSYCHOLOGIST IN A RESEARCH CENTER | 2

The following case gains interest from the close links between events in an organization and political trends outside it. In fact, this organization may be considered a political creation.

Our analysis is based on regular reports by a psychologist working in southern France. Although this is mainly a systemic interpretation of the psychologist's experiences, we will also look at the effects of an intervention we proposed to try to change an apparently hopeless situation from within.

HISTORY OF THE INSTITUTION

The institution we studied is a consultative body set up by the government of a large French town. It was founded in the 1960s as the Municipal Center for Pedagogic Analysis (MCPA).[1] Its *declared aim* was to elaborate "alternative" techniques for teachers in municipal night schools, whose students were all workers seeking primary- or secondary-school certificates.

The *nondeclared aim* was to create a local body through which Party A—then the majority political party in France—could control and direct the growing desire for change among rank-and-file teachers.

Here we can already discern an interesting phenomenon common in public social-service departments: the multiplicity and sometimes contradictory character of their aims. On the one hand, the officially stated objectives are intended in general to satisfy the demands of the public. On the other hand, implicit objectives are aimed at keeping the party in power and preserving the status quo; this is usually done by polarizing the political and cultural atmosphere, and then stressing the need to remain "in control" of any conflicts within the electorate. The ethical problems of this approach will not be discussed here—we want merely to draw attention to their existence, and to emphasize that they are bound to have adverse effects on psychologists and teachers involved in this type of institution. Moreover, they are bound to disrupt communications, both within the organization, and between it and the outside world.

Changing names in order not to change facts

In the early seventies, the institution changed its name to In-Service Training Center (INSET)—demonstrating the truism that changes in name may not involve genuine structural changes. At the same time, the director, the psychologist Professor Bariaud, was replaced by a younger, more dynamic man, a specialist in education, Professor Fontaine. The following reasons were given for this apparently radical change:

- The youth protest movement that exploded in French universities in May 1968 had brought a desire for profound changes among university lecturers and schoolteachers alike. The MCPA had shown itself incapable of absorbing these new ferments and revolutionary impulses.

- The rise of the popular left-wing Party B called for a new body —still controlled by Party A—capable of opposing the rising party in the educational sphere.

- The evident decline, over several years, in the activities of the MCPA was accompanied by a decrease in its influence on the public.

These factors, along with the need for a more efficient service, persuaded the local leaders of Party A to found a radically new service.

The new structure was more complex and more closely articulated than the old, with new sections for professional development, applied research, television, and computers. Each was headed by a specialist with a good university degree or professional qualifications.

It happened that Professor Bariaud, the former director of the MCPA, became the head of the professional development section, surrounding himself with a faithful band of former colleagues. Now, his new section made up a substantial part of INSET; indeed, at the beginning, 70 percent of its human and economic resources were allotted to the professional development section. This simple fact contained the seeds of a clash between the former director and his successor.

INSET's objectives

The *explicit* objectives of INSET were:

- To provide the school system of the town of XY with a consultative body.

- To organize a highly qualified municipal service for the training of permanent staff.

- To guarantee the high quality of the educational programs and institutions of the town.

- To help promote educational initiatives at the municipal level.

Every section of the center had clearly defined aims. Thus, the professional development section under Professor Bariaud was to organize lectures and training activities for municipal employees (especially for teachers at nursery and primary schools).

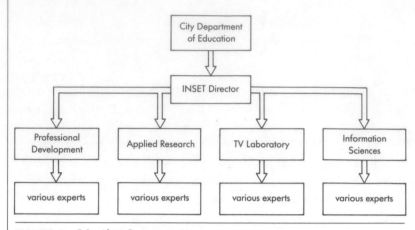

FIGURE 6a. Manifest Structure

The section devoted to applied research, led by Professor Louvoisier, had the task of designing a progressive education policy, developing new teaching techniques, and leading research on social topics. The television laboratory, run by M. Mounon, an expert in the field, had the double task of filming the center's activities and of providing audio-visual materials for schools.

The *implicit* objectives of the center, by contrast, were:

- To temper the urge of many educators to jettison prevailing instructional methods. To that end, the leadership of INSET proposed a "scientific" elaboration of the new ideas that had begun to captivate teachers, hoping thus to contain these ideas.

- To provide an apparently neutral body to enable Party A to counter the challenge of Party B in the field of education.

The lack of real change

Within this body, as in so many others connected with the public sector, a *latent structure* (Figure 6b) was in conflict with the *manifest structure* (Figure 6a). In other words, the official organizational

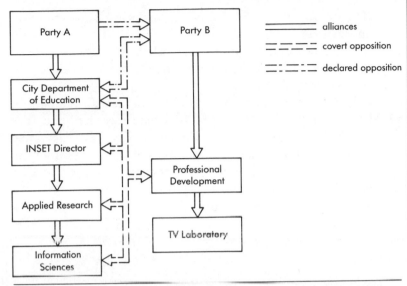

FIGURE 6b. Latent Structure

chart of INSET did not reflect the real balance of forces among its members.

The clash between the latent structure and the manifest structure came about because there were many contradictory aims (on the explicit and the implicit level) and because there were actually two centers of power (Fontaine, the new director; and Bariaud, now in charge of the section on professional development).

Because of political pressures, which were then quite acute, government bodies at all levels often created costly institutions devoted to change, such as INSET. But these bodies, having no power independent of the authorities that created them, were frequently handicapped by internal power struggles. The upshot was a reinforcement of the status quo.

If we take an insider's view of the MCPA, we see that its reorganization and its changed objectives simply reflected changes in the society (the rebellions of May 1968, concomitant changes in social values, the challenge by youth, the local political shift towards the left).

Thus we see that an institution can radically change its objectives and structure if that will ensure its survival—the homeostatic level of this type of institution is extremely high in the defense of its own existence. Clearly, this organization was able "to change in order not to change."

All communications within the center and with the outside world were bound to have unspoken overtones. Because there were many conflicting objectives, even the vocabulary was deliberately equivocal. Thus though different members of the center used the same terminology, the semantic and pragmatic content of that terminology differed.

Inevitably, this confusion affected the public as "users" of the system, users who expected clarity and "scientific certainty" from the experts at the center.

THE PSYCHOLOGIST IS CALLED IN

To illustrate the above analysis, let us briefly examine the method used to hire a psychologist at INSET.

Before choosing one, Professor Fontaine asked Professor Louvaine, director of the University Institute of Psychology, to recommend someone who was both highly qualified and politically reliable. His choice was Mlle. Lanzi.

In May 1972, the situation at INSET was as follows: Professor Fontaine had recently been asked by Party A and by the city government to restructure the center, which had hitherto been run "from behind the scenes" by a psychologist, Professor Bariaud. Professor Fontaine was expected to set up a central directorate, and to recruit psychologists, educators, communications experts, librarians, etc.

During his first meeting with Mlle. Lanzi, Professor Fontaine exclaimed, "You know, in this organization one has to accept a lot of aggravation. It's an interesting job, but very tiring. You will be expected to work the full eighteen hours a week on which your pay is based, unlike some others"—a reference to the psychologist Bariaud—"who are paid for forty hours but put in only ten. This is a responsible position, Mlle. Lanzi; don't let me down. I am counting on you, and on your colleague Professor Louvoisier, whom I know very well. You know how things were here in the past; I badly need help if everything is to run smoothly. That means keeping an eye on the people we've inherited. Some of them"— another reference to Professor Bariaud—"are used to doing just as they please and will simply have to be made to toe the line. I beg you again, Mlle. Lanzi—don't make me lose face. I'm counting on you." Such "advice" was repeated many times before the psychologist was officially hired as a consultant.

Hiring a partner for a coalition

Professor Fontaine's method of communication revealed the weakness of his position, especially with respect to Professor Bariaud. He tried to lead Mlle. Lanzi into a tacit coalition against Bariaud, whose influence over his colleagues Fontaine had good reason to fear. This corroborates our general finding that the hiring of a psychologist is often dictated by someone who feels insecure in his organization. Such appointments are always presented as *alliances for* something when in fact they are *coalitions against* an adversary in the institution.

Requests "for the sake of others"

Moreover, the hiring of psychologists is often presented as a *request for others rather than for oneself.* A teacher's appeal to a school psychologist for help in controlling a difficult pupil is a classic example. It is a request *for the sake of others* at the verbal level, but a request *for oneself* at the nonverbal, analogic level.

The result is a *paradoxical request,* made on two incompatible levels. The paradox springs from the impossibility of satisfying both levels at once. In fact, the two levels belong to different logical classes, two different hierarchies, inasmuch as a teacher's implicit request *for himself* is presented as an explicit request *for others.* As a result, the psychologist is driven into a corner:

- The psychologist cannot refuse the request.

- If the psychologist tries to deal only with the teacher's implicit request, he risks being rejected by the teacher ("But I came here to discuss the problems of my pupils . . .").

- If he accepts the explicit request, he is tacitly accepting the teacher's definition of the relationship and therefore loses the authority to construct a consultative context.

It follows that the psychologist must either grasp the paradoxical nature of the request from the outset, or else end up satisfying only the explicit request and thus disappointing the petitioner—and himself.

In any event, Mlle. Lanzi should have clarified her position right away, while giving a positive connotation to Professor Fontaine's appeal. She could have done this by saying, "I am most grateful for your interest and obvious kindness. I hope you will feel free to continue pointing me in the right direction." That sort of constructive but noncommital comment might well have persuaded Professor Fontaine to think again.

Her error was generated by her unusually strong dependence on Professor Fontaine, which limited her power to negotiate a proper contract.

Who is the real client?

A systemic analysis of the In-Service Training Center thus reveals that the psychologist was faced with great initial difficulties.

To begin with, she found it difficult to discover the real purpose of her post. Should she aim for the explicit or the implicit objectives, or for both at once?

She could not even tell by what criteria her professional work would be judged—by her fulfillment of the explicit (professional) objectives or the implicit ones (essentially political)?

Nor can a psychologist in her situation really tell who the actual *client* is. Is it the political appointee (in this case Professor Fontaine) or "the others" (child, teacher, school)—or both at once but at two distinct levels of intervention?

This confusion in definition is bound to make it extremely difficult to operate effectively. Yet it seems inevitable when the person hiring the psychologist is a politician or a senior bureaucrat.

All this creates difficult working conditions for the psychologist. Thus "the others," the ultimate users, may not be interested in what contribution the psychologist has to offer; the value of his work may be disparaged by the clients ("It costs us nothing, so it can't be much good"); he may suffer from the provisional nature of his position or from the lack of a proper professional context. He may be handicapped by his political dependence on the person who appointed him, or by the official's failure to appreciate the psychologist's results—as if to tell him, "I have appointed you not for what you can do, but simply to be able to tell the voters that we have a psychologist on staff."

The psychologist has a history of his own

It must be stressed that in general the psychologist *himself plays an active role in his own appointment.* When considering an institution with its own rules, history, and relational games, we must not forget that the psychologist has his own accumulation of experiences, errors and successes, concepts and ideologies, expectations and aims, and professional and economic interests.

In his first contacts with an institution, the psychologist may pay almost exclusive attention to the behavioral communications of his interlocutors and ignore his own. Moreover, he will often handle the interviews and the first phases of the new work in his own style, with familiar stratagems or relational tactics. He tends to introduce into the new working context the methods that have succeeded in other situations.

This approach is likely to foster initial errors that are bound to compromise his future work in the new situation. The strategies appropriate to one context are not necessarily appropriate to another.

Mlle. Lanzi's main mistake was her failure to agree on a period of preliminary observation with Professor Fontaine before arranging a work schedule. Moreover, the professional and economic importance she attached to his proposal led her to discount the importance of "details," only to discover their enormous relevance when it was too late.

These observations highlight the need for the psychologist to *adjust his own relational behavior,* above all while starting to work in a new institution. The psychologist must be able to adapt old methods to the new context, and to invent tactics and strategies of communication in keeping with the rules of the new system, while studying the system at close quarters. We will return to this topic in Part Two.

HOMEOSTASIS AND CHANGE

The objective of INSET is change

The events we have described could also have been presented from the viewpoint of the larger system—the municipal administration. Seen in that light, the creation of INSET played the important role of controlling the initiatives from below that made themselves felt after May 1968. It seemed a good idea to overhaul the old MCPA and to equip it with the latest trappings of modernity (television laboratory, specialized library, etc.) in order to ward off accusations of being out of date.

To that end, INSET advocated the continuing education of teachers to increase their awareness of their educational responsibilities and to increase their professional ability to tackle educational tasks.

As a result, the most prominent section was the one charged with the training of staff, directed by Professor Bariaud. Other sections gravitated to it, most noticeably the applied research section, created expressly to experiment with new educational methods and materials.

INSET may accordingly be described as a *structure set up to produce change,* as a kind of "leaven" amid the more or less inert and confused mass of teachers. It saw itself as a center of innovation and transformation, attentive to the signals emitted from below, ready to decode them and to intervene accordingly.

The reality of INSET is impotence

The absurdity of these pretensions and the extent to which they reflected the external political situation can be seen from the course INSET took following the local elections of May 1974, which marked an ostensibly important political change. These elections were won by Party B, which with Party C (also of the left) formed a new municipal administration. Party A was forced into opposition for the first time in many years.

Party B appointed Dr. Aubier head of the Department of Education. He was a political independent, who before the elections had acquired some notoriety in the small Party D. His appointment was made in recognition of the large number of votes he had mustered. This political gesture enabled Party B, now in power, to pause while it reflected on further initiatives.

According to the local press, Dr. Aubier's appointment was provisional and temporary. It was an excellent tactic both for Party B and for Dr. Aubier. Party B gained because the new head held no real political power, since the teachers' union opposed him. He was therefore quite unable to make real changes that might reflect badly on the party. For Dr. Aubier, the appointment at long last "offered a place at the head table," as the local paper put it.

After a few months Party B decided to replace Dr. Aubier, as soon as possible. The teachers' union hailed this position in its bulletin. But Dr. Aubier was absolutely determined not to leave office. The result was a stalemate between Dr. Aubier and Party B.

The INSET Center as a "project factory"

Let us now look at the effects inside INSET. It had just initiated a program for training kindergarten and nursery-school teachers. But upon his nomination, Dr. Aubier froze all projects until such time as they were "properly structured and fully thought out." The members of the center accepted this enforced pause gladly, since it would help them to examine their subjects in greater depth. They decided that their first objective must be to draw up a plan of action by January 1975.

After a great deal of thought, an outline plan was adopted and forwarded to the Department of Education on the agreed-upon date. It contained detailed proposals for resuming the training program, which had been interrupted in September. Several weeks passed, with no response. After numerous requests from the head of the center, the Department of Education said that the plan had been accepted in principle but that several details had still to be agreed on. And since the end of the school year was approaching, it would be best to wait for fall.

A new date was set: the revised plan was to be submitted by June 1975. The INSET staff went back to work, this time with obvious disappointment, and eventually came up with the required details.

During that period, various types of behavior were reported. Some reactions were depressive ("What on earth are we doing here?"); others were aggressive ("The department is taking us for a ride; we ought to tell them off"); some were moralistic and self-recriminating ("Is it right to take money for doing next to nothing month after month?"). In June 1975 two members resigned, declaring in an open letter that their position had become morally untenable. The rest engaged in long, useless arguments, an indication that they were under severe stress.

Nevertheless, by summer several projects had been drawn up. In September, the chairman of the Department of Education had not yet roused himself to action, merely informing the head of INSET that it lacked funds for the project. It was, however, a good idea, according to the department, to scale down last summer's program, particularly since the school year had just started and there was still plenty of time to review matters.

At this point the projects drawn up by INSET were broken down into numerous miniprojects, every participant doing his utmost to justify his continued presence—and salary. Four psychologists and teachers resigned. The director of the center threatened to do likewise, citing the intolerable political and professional situation.

The psychological climate at INSET rapidly deteriorated: morale plummeted, and there was constant bickering and bitterness about the futility of public institutions.

In January, Dr. Aubier called for a new set of "updated programs" for the next school year. These were submitted and duly filed away with all the old projects. At this point, the center was described by its own staff as "nothing more than a project factory."

The situation did not improve until the municipal council was reorganized. This led to Dr. Aubier's replacement at the Department of Education by a stable and efficient chairman, a leading member of Party B.

The era of projects came to an end, and the center gradually, though with difficulty, got back in harness.

Rank-and-file teachers had been agitating for several months for the revival of the refresher training course. Moreover, groups of teachers had banded together to run training activities in private centers, outside the control of the Department of Education. As one official explained, "That was the main reason why the authorities had to act at last."

Our examination of this affair led us to the conclusions that follow.

The paradoxical character of INSET

The situation at INSET during the time under review was clearly paradoxical. Founded expressly to inaugurate change, it was in fact used to maintain the status quo. In the process, energy and resources were wasted on unattainable projects—the projects themselves were all that changed.

This paradoxical situation, engendered by the proliferation of unrealized plans, was characterized not only by factional struggles over specific projects, but also by pathological symptoms (depression, aggression, guilt) in various individuals.

The institutional symptoms

This situation confirms the observation that perturbations outside an organization force it to change internally—and also create tension, sometimes to the point of collapse.

The energies of INSET, instead of being directed at greater productivity, were aimed exclusively at the internal environment, with destructive consequences. The institution nearly exhausted itself behaving as a closed system, with a crippling increase in entropy. This suggests the following conclusion: *When an institution confines its human, social, and economic resources to the intra-institutional environment, it tends to become dysfunctional and sterile.*

The endless meetings, the interminable discussions, the publication of documents and refutations, the motions, the projects, the organization's tedious self-analysis—these left little room for positive action. This sort of behavior, which can be described as *institutional symptoms,* presents psychologists with many signals about the functional level of an organization.

We can take it as an operational fact that, whenever the time and energy spent on internal affairs (meetings, elaboration of projects, verification of professional roles) account for more than a third of total work time, significant entropy has started, diverting energy from the productive flow of information between the institution and its true clients.

Changes at the top may provide satisfaction

A systemic analysis of the events engendered by the replacement of the chairman of the Department of Education is in order here.

Party B was pleased to have one of its own politicians in an influential position. Nor was Party A disappointed, since Professor Fontaine remained director of the In-Service Training Center.

After meetings with Party A and Party B, Professor Fontaine agreed to withdraw his proffered resignation, provided he "was left to work in peace and quiet." In concrete terms this meant the removal of Professor Bariaud and his allies from the center. It also meant a redefinition of the working methods at INSET: the old, rigid compartmentalization would make way for joint projects, each coordinated and directed by a team of experts drawn from the center itself and from outside.

Professor Fontaine was satisfied that he would now be able to "systemize" the service and to wield effective power over it as director.

Furthermore, Professor Bariaud and his "allies" made no fuss over their dismissal, as they had been invited to set up a new regional consulting center.

The new chairman of the Department of Education, too, was pleased with the course of events because he had been able to appoint new experts at INSET who were sympathetic to the educational policy of his party.

Last but not least, the "old" experts were satisfied because their work on concrete, feasible projects was being resumed, and because Professor Fontaine remained their director.

The grandiose projects developed by Professor Bariaud were abandoned; a concrete working plan was launched and quickly approved by both the chairman of the Department of Education and the trade unions. Its declared aim was to meet long-standing demands of rank-and-file teachers.

Chain reactions and polystability of the system

The effects of changes in the chairmanship of the Department of Education support the systemic axiom that *real changes at any level of a system induce changes at all other levels of the system.* In other words, the entire system is thereby restructured, with a concomitant modification of the method of information exchange with the environment.

As in astrophysics, so too in our case: "Disequilibrium can become a source of order" (Prigogine, Morin). Throughout all its changes and mutations, INSET remained "polystable" and "homeokinetic," that is, capable of possessing an equilibrium that changes temporarily (Beer; Iberall et al.).

In such changing situations, the psychologist's room for intervention is restricted and subject to more closely coordinated methods. In our case, the "intervening subsystem" was made up of a group of experts of equal status—our research group. One of our objectives was to tackle the complex problem of communication, and especially of communication with the final users (the teachers taking refresher courses).

Denied coalitions and disrupted communications

We have seen that the institution under review had numerous explicit and implicit objectives, often mutually incompatible. This led to incompatibilities between the official and the latent structure, and encouraged the emergence of endemic conflicts. Let us now see how this affected the methods of communication used by members of INSET.

Disruptions of communication were inevitable, since the very method by which members of the staff were recruited and appointed to the center triggered a dysfunctional response. The nominees were implicitly expected to belong to the two main political parties—in equal proportions. Thus if an expert from Party A was appointed for one project, a member of Party B had to be chosen for the next, and so on.

This method of power-sharing is, of course, hardly confined to France. This basic institutional "rule," known by all but never discussed, assumes the impossibility of arriving at real agreement or of transcending the calls of party. Moreover, in this context of formal agreement and underlying hostility, internal communications were never "read" for what they were, but as expressions of party affiliation. The result at INSET was that implicit meanings were read into the statements of all members.

Hence, implicit (but unacknowledged) *coalitions* arose between persons of one political ideology *against* persons perceived as belonging to the opposite ideology. This explains why ideological "identities" were so often attributed to people who did not feel bound by them. The upshot was a clear opposition of "identities" within the different groups of the organization.

It is interesting to note that this opposition was mainly expressed nonverbally: with a barely noticeable smile, a wink, a frown, a lifting of the eyebrows when a political opponent spoke, a whisper, a particular tone of voice when replying to an "adversary"; an oblique remark to refute an argument.

The myth of agreement at any price

Explicitly, of course, hostility was disavowed, in keeping with the widespread belief that all members of an efficient department must agree on methods and objectives.

In our case, this "myth of agreement at any price" served to cover up the structural hostility between staff members. However, the myth itself was implicit: had it been put into words, it would immediately have been denied and disavowed.

This situation resembles the pseudoreciprocal dynamics of families with a schizophrenic member (described by L. Wynne and Thaler Singer). Pseudoreciprocal relationships are often covered by a facade of harmony which actually hides a shared attempt to overcome the underlying feelings of emptiness, incoherence, and meaninglessness.

Conflict in social institutions is not necessarily dysfunctional; indeed, it can reflect the vitality of explicitly acknowledged crosscurrents, so long as it is not excessive. However, *conflict is always disruptive when its existence is denied.* The inevitable consequence is a breakdown in communications.

Identical words for different subjects

Let us now describe a meeting held in September 1977 by the team (including our psychologist) charged with organizing a training program for kindergarten teachers.

The agenda included reviewing a bibliography intended for the leaders of all the groups involved in the training program. The meeting began with an invitation by the chairman to suggest suitable works on education, psychology, and preschool education.

At one point, after proposing a long list of books and papers, someone declared that not only the team but the teachers, too, ought to read all the recommended literature if they wanted to be up to date. This suggestion was endorsed by the majority, the members soon competing with one another in bringing up further texts and authors, in examining their theoretical foundations, and so forth.

The rest of the meeting was devoted to a discussion of two distinct subjects (a bibliography for the group leaders and one for the kindergarten teachers), which were, however, treated as if they were the same thing.

The result was confusion and a general lack of understanding: a flood of names, voices and sounds, several persons speaking at once, a desperate attempt by the chairman to reach a consensus, and more than half the group complaining of headaches. Needless to say, no definitive bibliography was agreed on.

Different words for the same subject

A similar situation occurred at a later meeting about the kindergarten teachers' program. Each expert was asked to deal with a specific aspect of the scheme. One hotly contested issue was the method of evaluating the training program at its end. Though the various experts spoke of the same subject and were in substantial agreement, they adopted different terms to refer to it, and so laid the foundation for future misunderstandings. The terms used were "verification," "evaluation," and "comprehension."

Now, these distinct terms for the same thing clearly reflected the ideological differences of the various experts. It was also clear that the inevitable cliques and coalitions had their roots in the

Department of Education, since its (politically appointed) chairman appointed all the members.

THE RESEARCH GROUP PROPOSES A REMEDY

This situation was analyzed and discussed in depth by our research group. We eventually decided that the best way to repair the apparently hopeless state of affairs was for the psychologist, with caution and delicacy, at an appropriate moment to *give a positive connotation to the differences in the conceptual models used by the various experts and then to help them accept the differences frankly.*

During a working session, then, the psychologist described the implicit assumptions (known to all) and proposed that those present proceed to analyze the differences between the various models. The *declared* aim was to examine the results produced by each one of the models at the end of the training period and to discover their *common elements.*

The first result was to improve the flow of communication by explicating the differences in the various models. True, the unacknowledged coalitions continued in force, as did the myth of mutuality; it proved impossible to do anything about them because they were rooted in the very existence of the organization.

We wish to stress, however, that although we were dealing with a conflict, the situation was not yet severe enough to be apparent to the final users or to lead to the end of the training program. In general, the breakdown in communications, like dysfunctions in the internal environment, must cross a critical threshold before it becomes obvious, either by its intensity or by its persistence, to the client. This threshold plainly varies from system to system.

TWO PSYCHOLOGISTS IN A PEDIATRICS WARD 3

The following events involve a particular but by no means exceptional situation, that of a psychologist joining one institution to do research on behalf of another.

The research (into the response of children to hospitalization and the resulting relationship between their families and the hospital) was done in the pediatrics department of a city hospital in central Italy. The project, funded by the city, was conducted by two psychologists attached to a university institute in the same city.

Although the two psychologists subscribed to the systemic model and thus should have known better, they had made the initial error of failing to define their precise standing in the hospital, and hence had failed to devise an appropriate strategy. In other words, while they thought they were adopting a systemic model, they were, in fact, assuming that the system being observed (the pediatrics department and its interactions with the patients' families) was one of fixed relationships which their presence would not affect.

In keeping with established practice, the research project was launched after discussions between the director of research, the psychologists, and the head of the department—without consulting the doctors and nurses. We shall return to this point and its practical effects.

For the moment, let us stress that, from the first, the psychologists were faced with an unexpected series of requests and communications from members and subgroups in the department. These were unsolicited and seemed to arise simply because the psychologists were there.

The compass of these appeals made the psychologists wonder whether they should continue to collect information while ignoring the interactions between the *observing system* and the *observed system.*

It became clear that the problem had to be solved when the psychologists realized that their presence in the department had created a situation that impeded the collection of information and, worse, tended to render it unreliable.

At this point the psychologists confided their doubts to our research group. They asked, "Can we go on isolating our research from its context, in the name of scientific objectivity? Or is it possible—even essential—to study the effects of our contacts with the various subsystems at the hospital?"[1]

Our group, having examined the situation, thought it worthwhile to analyze the hospital context where our two psychologists had begun their research, with a view toward modifying that context at a later stage.

NATURE OF THE RESEARCH PROJECT

Before examining the interaction between the psychologists and the pediatrics department, let us first look more closely at the research project itself. Its specific objective was the analysis of children's reactions to hospitalization and the relationship between their families and the pediatrics department.

This emphasis distinguished the project from many previous ones. Most studies of the hospitalization of children have dealt with children deprived of maternal care—studies very much in vogue after the Second World War, especially in Britain. In these studies the problem was viewed almost exclusively as a problem of mother-child separation, especially in the work of J. Bowlby and J. Robertson, who in 1952 focused attention on the effects of hospitalization on the mental health of children. In particular, collaborating with the Child Development and Research Unit in the Tavistock Clinic and the Tavistock Institute of Human Relations, they studied the behavior of children during hospitalization and following their release.[2]

Bowlby and Robertson concluded that the temporary separation of children from their mothers, as in traditional hospitalization, could be so traumatic for young children as to upset mental health permanently. They found that the problem vanished when the mother-child bond was not disrupted and the mother was hospitalized with her child.

It is true that recent critiques of the maternal-deprivation concept basic to these investigations, and of the methodological limitations that restricted the investigation to the mother and child, thus excluding any other significant variables, have rather diminished the credibility of this approach.[3] Nonetheless, these studies caused quite a stir at the time, and they opened the way, especially in Britain, for the practice of "rooming in"—letting mothers stay in the hospital with their children.

The present research project, though, was guided by different considerations. The problem of child hospitalization was examined in a wider context. Thus, while not neglecting the problem of the mother-child relationship, the team also considered all other relationships in the family system as well as the interactions between the family system and the pediatrics department during the child's stay in the hospital.

In terms of general systems theory, the family and the pediatrics department can be considered "open systems"—that is, "organized complexities" that continuously exchange information with the environment. Viewed in this light, the hospital is not so much a place where the mother-child bond is broken, as a place where two systems, the family and the pediatrics department, meet and interact, and where there is the constant possibility of conflict due to the different rules governing the two systems. It follows that the behavior of the hospitalized child can largely be attributed to developing interactions in each system and also between the two systems.

Our research project was meant to verify our working hypothesis that the relations between the child's family and the pediatrics department, as well as the child's own reactions to hospitalization, depend directly on the characteristics of the family group. According to the typology proposed by Minuchin (1967 and 1974), these characteristics must be distributed over a continuum, with an "enmeshed" family at one end and a "disengaged" family at the other.

Between the pediatrics department and the enmeshed family there often develops a competitive (symmetrical) type of relationship based on the claim of each side that it has an exclusive claim to the patient. For such a family (characterized by the feeling that all the needs of a family member can and should be satisfied inside the family), a pediatrician's claim to be solely responsible for the sick child is a direct challenge, likely to engender symmetrical escalations.

The relationship between the disengaged family and the pediatricians, by contrast, is built on complementary lines, characterized by the family's acceptance of its own lack of competence and a willingness to entrust the care of the patient to specialists. Given the attitude of many pediatrics departments, these families will often end up relinquishing all responsibility; in this case the relationship between the family and the department is said to be "metacomplementary"—the family in effect encourages the department to adopt a cavalier attitude towards it.

These differences are bound to affect the sick child's behavior. Sick children from enmeshed families can be expected, because of the competitive relationship between the family and the department, to show pathological signs described by Bowlby and Robertson as characteristic of the "protest" and "despair" phases. Children from disengaged families should from the very first show signs of adapting to the new environment, an attitude Bowlby and Robertson consider characteristic of the final phase of "detachment."

These hypotheses concern the content of the research project, though in what follows we shall be dealing not with that subject but with the problems involved at a different logical level, that of "metaresearch." All the same, we feel it would be useful to look briefly at the subject of the research itself, the better to demonstrate how research impinges on a theme closely involved in the conflicts of institutions. This involvement occurs for at least two reasons:

- The family-hospital relationship is a permanent focus of rivalry (like the family-school relationship), because both systems are institutionally responsible for the same subject, namely the child. Moreover, the study in question explored the family-hospital, or client-service, relationship in Italy at a time when hospitals had lost some of their credibility and demands for client control were increasing.

- The second reason is largely ideological. In Italy, the idea of having mothers "room in" with their hospitalized children, first proposed in British studies, is a political issue (cf. Maccacaro).

Inasmuch as they interrupt the bonds between mother and child, pediatrics wards have been accused of hiding their violent nature behind a benevolent face, much like psychiatric hospitals. The pediatrician himself has been described as someone who, by removing the mother, "holds sway over a medical science of objects"—persons treated as things—"a science in the service of capitalism" (Maccacaro). This is not the place to analyze this thesis, which is open to argument. We want only to draw attention to the ideological background of this field of research, and to the inevitable formation of antagonistic positions.

THE RESEARCHERS JOIN THE PEDIATRICS DEPARTMENT: INITIAL ERRORS

Our study called for the psychologists to work in a pediatrics ward for several months. This raised the problem of defining their relationship with the various subsystems of the hospital.

As research by J. Haley, G. Bateson, P. Watzlawick, and others at the Mental Research Institute in Palo Alto has shown, every human interaction involves a series of consciously or unconsciously framed messages defining the nature of the relationship between the subjects of the interaction. Every communication thus carries, over and above the *informational* aspect of the message, a *relational* aspect that defines the relationship between the subjects. Even if all messages do not have contents of equal importance, they all serve to define relationships. Thus, if A says to B, "I am tired today," he does more than describe his subjective state and transmit information; he implicitly says to B, "Do something for me," or at least, "Adopt an attitude acknowledging my fatigue." In any case, A's message will in some way tend to define his relationship with B.

The process of defining the implied relationship between interacting subjects is always mutual, inasmuch as neither party can impose his definition on the other. Every message is in fact a means of proposing a definition of a relationship, a proposal that can be confirmed, rejected, or disqualified by the recipient. Both *complementary* and *symmetrical* relationships are possible.

> A complementary relationship is one where the two people are exchanging different types of behaviors. One gives and the other receives, one teaches and the other learns. The two people exchange behavior which complements, or fits together. One is in a "superior" position and the other in an "inferior" position, in the sense that one criticizes and the other accepts it, one offers advice and the other follows it, and so on.[4]

When, by contrast, an exchange of messages is based on equality or near-equality, then the behavior of one participant tends to reflect that of the other, and we have what is called a symmetrical interaction.

Normally, a relationship, whether complementary or symmetrical, also involves exchanges of messages contrary to the predominant relational scheme (that is, symmetrical messages in complementary relationships, or the reverse). They have a self-regulating effect on the relationship, and their absence leads to what Bateson has called "schismogenesis," defined as "the process of differentiation of the norms of individual behavior resulting from cumulative interaction between individuals."[5]

Schismogenesis in a complementary relationship causes one of the two interacting subjects or groups to become increasingly active and dominant while the other tends to become increasingly passive and submissive. Schismogenesis in a symmetrical relationship, by contrast, will step up the competition until it explodes. It should also be noted that when the problems in the definition of a relationship increase, the informational content of a message tends to lose its importance; all that matters is control of the definition of the relationship.

The context in which a relationship develops both defines the nature of the various messages and restricts the degree of freedom of the subjects in the definition of their relationship. The hierarchic structure of an organization, for example, tends to determine the relationships between its members, much as certain cultures define the master-pupil and doctor-patient relationships as complementary.

In our specific case, many factors imposed limitations on the definition of the psychologists' relationship with the different subsystems of the organization. Among these were their having to ask a hospital department for permission to pursue their research, their membership in a university department, their professional qualifications as psychologists, and the involvement of the city administration as a silent partner in their project.

Thus, since the two psychologists had not been called in by the pediatrics department, they were unable to set the rules defining the relationship. They ought to have found some means of controlling the relationship, if only to create a collaborative context in which to pursue their work. But they failed to do this during their first contacts with the department.

The psychologists did manage to enlist the support of the chief of pediatrics, but failed to involve the related subsystems.

At a meeting between the psychologists and the chief of pediatrics, the subject of the research was discussed in a somewhat summary fashion. The chief physician continually turned the conversation to other, more general subjects. On that occasion, the research team asked for meetings with the medical and nursing staff in order to enlist their cooperation, but the chief brushed these requests aside—since the team had his full support, they might just as well start the very next day. It was not until later and after much prodding on their part that he allowed the psychologists to hold a meeting with the medical staff.

On that occasion, two members of the hospital staff—a young pediatrician who was also a specialist in psychology, and a social worker who, one year before, had polled the views of doctors and nurses on the question of mothers staying in the hospital—tried to establish a coalition with the psychologist. The meeting ended with peremptory instructions by the chief physician: all those present had to collaborate in the project. Our psychologists had failed to remove the obstacles set up by the chief, and hence could not win the rest of the department over to their project. When the project was officially launched, by handing out questionnaires to the parents of hospitalized children, it became immediately clear that, because the psychologists had failed to define the relationship, the hospital staff defined it themselves on the basis of previous experiences with psychologists.

Although the psychologists had said nothing to justify this assumption, the staff of the pediatrics department were convinced that the researchers were in favor of mothers staying in the ward. Another deeply rooted prejudice was the assumption that the research would conclude with a sharp attack on the department. This explains why the psychologists continually got apologetic messages from the medical and nursing staff, along with anxious requests for information about the parents' views. These anxieties reflected the fact that the research project was financed by the city; it was suspected that the research team was checking up on the hospital. This mistaken view was based on earlier experiences, particularly with a graduate student from the same university, whose studies in the department had culminated in a thesis with the polemical title, "The Hospital as a Traumatic Experience." That thesis had been used as a battering ram by a group of physicians in favor of mothers staying in the ward. Also, the accusations of a public action group of the extreme left, of which some psychologists were members, had disturbed the staff deeply. The group had also put up posters accusing the hospital of using children as guinea pigs.

To sum up, due to the errors of the psychologists themselves, and also to past experiences, many hospital employees looked on the research project with suspicion from the start.

The members of the pediatrics department, feeling that they were under scrutiny, reacted in two main ways: by giving only the minimum of information, and by trying to channel the anticipated negative connotations of the research towards the children's families, whom they blamed for most of the department's difficulties. Moreover, because they had rejected the masked offer to make common cause with a subgroup in the department (i.e., the young pediatrician and the social worker), the psychologists found that they were being isolated and that the pediatrics staff refused to give them any assistance.

It proved impossible to gather essential information about the stay of mothers in the department. The psychologists were told that the parents' visiting hours were the same as those of the general public, when in fact it was common to extend the parents' visiting hours sometimes to the point of allowing mothers to stay on around the clock. Against this background the two psychologists presented their predicament to our group.

A STRATEGY TO REDEFINE
THE PREVAILING RELATIONSHIP

It became clear that the psychologists had to redefine their relationship with the staff of the pediatrics department. Our group felt that many of the misunderstandings could be blamed on the psychologists' own mistakes. A chance to redefine their relationship came when the chief physician of the department was replaced by one of his former pupils.

The group stressed two aspects of the psychologists' current status:

- The psychologists joined the hospital not on their own behalf but on behalf of a wider system, namely the university center and the municipal council which financed the research. To redefine the relationship would therefore require the examination not only of the "observer-observed" system (in this case, the psychologists and the pediatrics department), but also of the supersystem (see Figure 7).

- The psychologists were not appointed by the hospital, but had asked permission to do research on behalf of another organization to which they were answerable. That situation implicitly defined the institution in which they did their research work as a mere "data bank," and hence created an atmosphere of noncooperation. To remedy this, the two psychologists would have to agree with the pediatrics staff as to which data they would be feeding back into the "data bank" at the end of their research. Only in that way could a real (not apparent) involvement of the staff be won. This step would, moreover, have to be part of a much wider plan for the

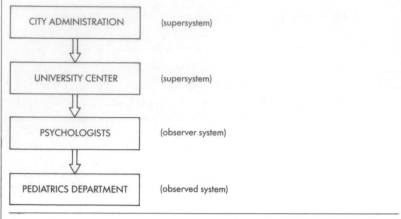

FIGURE 7.

redefinition of the relationship and of the hierarchic information channels.

Defining the relationship with the new chief physician

The university's director of research contacted the new chief of
pediatrics to ask if he would like the research to continue, deliberately avoiding any reference to the delicate subject of the psychologists' relationship with the former chief. The new man
expressed willingness to work with them, and the director of research arranged for him to meet the two psychologists, who
would explain their ideas in detail. During their meeting the new
chief proved to be so keen that the psychologists were afraid he
would try to take over the project. He nevertheless agreed that
the psychologists should hold separate meetings with the medical
and nursing staff, merely insisting that he must be present at all
their meetings with the physicians. He also insisted that these
meetings be held on Friday mornings, which he had specially set
aside for professional discussions with members of his medical
staff. In other words, he clearly wished to be seen as the leader of
the project.

As we came to realize later, the cordial behavior of the new
chief of pediatrics had two distinct motives:

- To demonstrate his readiness to discuss problems associated with children's diseases—including the topic of parents in the ward—thus scotching a current rumor to the contrary.

- To use this opportunity for improving relations with the university center. (He sought closer links because the university, barely touched by student revolt, had thus preserved its old prestige, and because the hospital was likely someday to be officially attached to the university.)

His willingness to collaborate was given a fresh boost by the tactics agreed to by our group and then used by the psychologists: (1) To dispel the widespread suspicion that the team was spying on behalf of the city by demonstrating that the connection between them was purely formal. (2) To demonstrate to the department the fundamental importance of the research project.

Now that the chief physician's objectives did not clash with the psychologists', the only difficulty was his insistence that he be present at all meetings with the medical staff. However, in view of his recent appointment and the inherent problems of starting in a new job, the group felt that it had gained as much as could be expected.

Redefining the relationship with the medical staff

To redefine their relationship with the medical staff, the psychologists had to dispel the impression that the project was intended to evaluate and judge. At their meetings with the doctors, they stressed that the involvement of the city government was purely formal and that they were not its agents. Verbally and nonverbally, they were careful to present themselves as complementary, or noncompetitive.

In meetings with physicians and with nurses, they repeatedly portrayed their requests for information as requests for help. In particular, they asked for help in interpreting data. They stressed that only the staff members were able render that help, because of their experience and qualifications.

These tactics not only dissolved old suspicions, but aroused active interest in the research project.

It should be noted, moreover, that the rivalry between the old and the new chief physicians (both attended the meetings), which took the form of a contest to see which was more "helpful," left the psychologists with a good deal of scope in running things.[6] The psychologists were careful not to become entangled in this rivalry, though they demonstrated at the nonverbal level that they considered the new chief the ultimate authority.

Redefinition of the relationship with the nursing staff

At first, the research team had completely ignored the nursing staff, to the point of failing to mention the project to them, even informally. Their approach had been identical to that of inexperienced family therapists who, in interacting with a family, accept the very "rules" that have caused the dysfunctions within the family. By failing to involve the lower levels of staff, they merely perpetuated the hospital system's tacit rule of consulting the paramedical staff only about routine tasks.

As a result, the nurses had become hostile to the research project. To remedy this, they were now invited to meetings to discuss ways of improving the flow of information.[7] These meetings were announced on the departmental bulletin board, and care was taken to emphasize how much the support of the nursing staff was needed and appreciated by the team, not least because they had the closest contacts with the patients and their families. These meetings, attended by a large number of nurses, were held in the absence of any members of a higher hierarchic level. This move facilitated a free exchange of views. (In fact, the doctors had absented themselves for political reasons: at the time, the nurses were agitating for better conditions, and the senior medical staff had begun to feel that their authority was being challenged.)

RESULTS OF REDEFINING THE RELATIONSHIP

The psychologists' redefinition of their relationship with the department led to radical changes. In particular, it helped them gather information they had been unable to obtain for four months, on

■   The relationship between the nursing staff and the families.

■   The behavior of the hospitalized children.

■   The attitude of the various professional categories to the overnight stay of mothers in the ward.

However, just as the psychologists were about to attain their objective, they realized that their data were bound up with departmental conflicts, so inextricably as to prevent any definition of the relationship between the hospital as a whole and the mothers of hospitalized children. For example, official visiting hours were set at two hours per day, but it was common for parents to stay the whole day, and for mothers to sleep in the ward regardless of their children's condition. This situation caused bad feelings all around; every member of the department felt free to advise families about visiting privileges, so that the parents often received highly contradictory messages. The result was constant friction between the doctors, the nurses, and the parents, the length of whose visits was regulated quite capriciously.

Parents who stayed beyond the official visiting hours suffered anxiety, for they were never sure whether they were allowed to stay by right or by special favor. Whenever they met staff members opposed to their staying, they were asked to leave, a request reinforced by a loudspeaker announcement every night. On the other hand, when they met sympathetic staff members, they were told that it was their right to stay—often that it was their moral duty.

The psychologists discovered that the matter was never discussed officially, and that all attempts to regularize parents' visits had failed. But in individual interviews with staff members, it emerged that opinions were not so divided as to prevent a compromise. The fact that they had not reached one showed that the content of the arguments had become of secondary importance. The arguments were simply being used as a *pretext for expressing the symmetrical opposition* of some groups to others. The interviews showed that staff members were more concerned with adopting attitudes than with solving the actual problem.

The nurses were opposed to long stays in the ward, since they had to bear the brunt of the mothers' presence. Even so, they contributed to the status quo, thanks to their symmetrical relationship with the doctors. The nurses felt that the medical staff took a permissive attitude to the parents simply to avoid unpleasant arguments, leaving it to them to perform the thankless task of ejecting them. They refused to play that game, adopting instead a symmetrical opposition to the doctors: "If they want to kowtow to the parents, we can be even sweeter." The two groups thus came to resemble each other when, in fact, they held quite distinct positions.

The left-wing physicians, who had been isolated by their colleagues, defended the protracted presence of parents in the wards largely for political reasons. They argued that parents were there by right and that the clients were the ultimate judges of the services they used. Contending that this problem had to be considered in conjunction with all the other organizational problems of the department, they called for joint meetings of doctors and nurses. This issue thus gave them a chance to unite against the new chief physician, who wanted to restrict parents' visits. The majority of their colleagues, though not opposed in principle to the parents' presence, objected to meeting the nursing staff on an equal footing and to the prospect of a total reorganization of the department. Thus, by calling for mixed meetings, the left-wing doctors tried to cement their alliance with the nurses, and to maintain their leading role in it.

The pediatrician who specialized in child psychology was also in favor of the parents' protracted stay in the ward. She was most concerned about the mental health of the children in the ward, and objected to the fact that "some people" had given the problem a political bias when the issue was simply a mother's duty to her child.

In this way, she opposed her left-wing colleagues, while presenting herself to the new chief physician as a possible adviser. Her object was an alliance with the new chief, in order to secure the position and prestige that the old chief had not granted her. To that end, she now softened her previously intransigent approach to the new chief. This made her a kind of "mediator" between him and the left-wing group.

The deputy chief physician generally favored the extended presence of parents, but thought their visits should be regulated in a way that met the psychological needs of the children but didn't hamper the management of the ward. He disapproved of the left-wing group's attempt to politicize the problem. Yet he also objected to the new chief's approach to the problem, and openly criticized it as an attempt to regiment the life of the department. He thus sought to increase his influence by challenging the professional and administrative leadership of his new chief.

The junior medical staff were largely indifferent to the problem. Though they were against the constant presence of parents in the ward on the grounds that it interfered with hospital routine, they presumed that the problem was insoluble because of the supposed irreconcilability between the smooth running of the department and the psychological needs of the hospitalized child. So they ignored the regulations proposed by the new chief. They praised his predecessor, though, who by virtue of great tolerance and subtlety didn't need to impose rigid rules about the length of time parents spent in the ward.

Only one physician was openly opposed to the round-the-clock stay of parents and demanded that the formal visiting hours be adhered to. He was an old friend of the pediatrics chief, and it was taken for granted that their views would be identical.

The new chief himself wasn't favorable to the constant presence of parents in the ward, but he quickly realized that an intransigent attitude might shake his authority. Soon after his arrival, the new chief had made an interim ruling about visiting hours, which was quietly ignored by the entire staff (including the former chief). The new chief soon rescinded it and learned to be more flexible toward the problem. However, he had no intention of entirely shelving his plan to regularize the matter, through which he meant to demonstrate his style of management and impose his authority over the paramedical staff—and even over the old chief.

The nursing staff, too, was divided. A small group of specialized nurses were allied with the left-wing doctors. They favored longer hours for parents in the ward, provided that they were officially endorsed in a meeting that included the nursing staff. The reason for this stipulation was that the burden of the longer hours inevitably fell on the nurses, not the doctors.

But the largest group of nurses were exasperated with both the parents and the doctors. They blamed doctors for encouraging parents to ignore the visiting hours while leaving the nurses to cope with the questions and complaints. They stressed that the constant presence of some parents interfered with proper nursing of the patients. These parents, instead of helping their children, kept telling the nurses what to do. For all these reasons, this group, while in favor of somewhat extended hours, decried the continuous presence of parents.

The nurses of the third group were opposed to any extension and called for the unequivocal restoration of the official hours. They complained of parents who behaved too aggressively towards them, and of doctors who sided with parents against the nurses.

The analysis of this data led to a fundamental conclusion: all research into the relationship between the families and the staff, and into the bearing of this relationship on the young patients, must also pay heed to the relationships among the various subgroups of the hospital staff.

Though a single experience does not allow one to generalize, we will suggest as a hypothesis that the *definition of a relationship* has such a strong determining effect on every interpersonal problem that ignoring it means running the risk of misinterpreting the data gathered.

INDIVIDUAL STAFF INTERVIEWS

Before discussing the psychologists' redefinition of the relationship between the various subgroups, we should point out that in the period directly following their new contract, the psychologists— according to their research program and in addition to group meetings—held individual interviews with each member of the medical and nursing staff. From them, the psychologists had hoped to obtain a clearer picture of staff attitudes towards the patients' families, and in particular toward the continuous presence of mothers in the ward. To that end, the interviews should have been carefully planned to explore areas not readily opened up by questionnaires. Because this was not done, the individual interviews went wrong from the start. Instead of providing specific information, they were occasions for venting frustration with the department. As a result, the interviews dragged on in a climate of increasingly bitter recrimination. The relationship between the staff and the parents, which ought to have been the central point of the agenda, had become a pretext for arguments about relationships within the department.

It should be observed from the individual interviews that such meetings with the members of an institution encourage the expression of grievances and relational tensions, particularly when the institution is torn by conflicts.

It is, moreover, quite possible that the psychologists, influenced by their desire to study the relational dynamics of the organization, had inadvertently encouraged the interviewers to express their "institutional suffering" by holding out the hope of a possible cure.

AN EMBARRASSING TURNABOUT

The psychologists' second research phase was designed to rescue them from their previous errors. The aim was to create an atmosphere of collaboration with the pediatrics department which would speed their collection of data. However, within a few weeks the psychologists found themselves in an opposite but no less embarrassing situation: they were shifted from the fringe to the center of the conflict by groups that saw them as an instrument for change.

New pressures, accompanied by overtures of alliance, were bound up with the department's factional game. Thus the new chief offered the psychologists his full support, in the form of special facilities and help with organizational difficulties, and expressed admiration for their work. In exchange, he expected their collaboration in his plan to regularize the stay of parents in the ward. He wanted them to persuade the doctors, especially the left-wing doctors, whose attitude he deplored. With the help of the psychologists, he also hoped to tighten links with the university center, thus paving the way for the transformation of his department into a branch of the university. This step would clearly have strengthened his standing in the hospital.

The left-wing doctors and nurses suggested that the psychologists help them improve the relationship between the doctors and nurses in the pediatrics department. In particular, they asked the psychologists to report their findings to combined meetings of doctors and nurses; they stressed the pedagogic and therapeutic impact that this approach would have on their colleagues and, above all, on the "boss."

The deputy chief physician made a frank appeal to the psychologists on behalf of the department, expressing the hope that, with the help of the information collected at the meetings, the team might come up with a diagnosis of the department's malaise. In his opinion it was all due to the failure of the new chief to run the department efficiently.

The pediatrician who specialized in child psychology, by contrast, gave them a copy of her own study on the attitude of the departmental staff to the patients' parents—a study that had been the basis of previous attempts to reorganize the department. In this way, she now tried to pass on to her "colleagues" in our team the role of reformer she had been unable to play.

Faced with all these demands and expectations, the psychologists realized that they had jumped out of the frying pan into the fire, from the fringe to center stage, from an "evaluative and judgmental" role to a "therapeutic" one that was clearly incompatible with their research.

REPORTING THE RESULTS OF THE RESEARCH PROJECT TO THE DEPARTMENT

Our research group discussed the second phase of the project at length. The cause of the radical change in the psychologists' position was, by common consent, found to be the individual interviews with the members of the department. Unfortunately, there was no way of determining what might have happened if they had not held these interviews.

Somebody concluded pessimistically that, with the current state of knowledge, it seemed inevitable that psychologists should find themselves either on the fringe or else at the very center of interdepartmental politics.

The research group also discussed its own influence on the two psychologists, who reported finding themselves in simultaneous interaction with two systems: the pediatrics department and the research group.

Looking back, we saw how our tendency to focus on relational games had led the psychologists to concentrate, during their interviews with the staff, not on their actual field of research, but on relational problems. The "invisible presence" of the research group, and the interaction between the psychologists and the pediatrics department, had produced a "game for three," whose effects are hard to evaluate.

Also, the research group agreed that the psychologists should ignore all requests for intervention by departmental subgroups— as researchers, they had no business intervening in the management of the department. Such intervention would be to confuse the research context with the therapeutic context, and hence, to commit new errors.

We therefore decided that the psychologists would simply present an "aseptic" synthesis of their data at a final meeting set aside for reporting their findings to the pediatrics department. If they were asked to intervene, they would not only decline, but also avoid any discussion of the conflicts in the department. By doing so, they would restore their role as research workers, though at the cost of disappointing various members and subgroups in the department. As it turned out, they disappointed quite a few.

4 | A TEAM OF EDUCATIONAL PSYCHOLOGISTS IN A SUBURBAN SCHOOL DISTRICT

The next case demonstrates how valuable detailed information about an institution can be to a psychologist about to join it. The preliminary information available was rather complex but, for that reason, proved most useful to the psychologist in devising an effective strategy. This is the only case discussed in this book in which the psychologist had the support of our research group from the start.

There are several reasons for including this case. First, it shows how much effort is needed to create a communication network free of repetitive circuits. Second, the team's approach was judged to be very positive by the users. Third, it provides a clear example that all practitioners will find of value. Our account will deal exclusively with the system constituted by the research team —a psychologist and a psychomotor therapist—and the school system in question, and with the tactics applied to prevent or remedy breakdowns in communication.

The psychologists' strategic and tactical moves reflected our group's systemic approach to the situation: the reader should note that what made it work was not verbal communication (overvalued in our culture) but the opposite—implicit, analogic, and behavioral forms of communication.

INFORMATION ABOUT THE CONTEXT

The government of an Italian provincial city received a request from a local school district for the services of a team of psychologists. It was one of three school districts surrounding the city, and it included several outlying suburbs. The request itself was not new. Various representatives from the school district (members of the parents' association, the director, and various teachers) had vainly been pressing the city administration for years to send them such a team. In fact, several psychologists had been assigned to the school district in the past, but they had been shared with other districts—which had since succeeded in getting the city to assign them a permanent team of psychologists. This development encouraged representatives of the schools under discussion to renew their request.

Previously, the city had blamed its failure to provide such a team on a shortage of professionals. However, when a special school was closed, a psychologist and a psychomotor therapist became available and agreed to be transferred. But they both felt somewhat apprehensive about the assignment. The school district was a considerable distance from the center of town, and its unwieldy size posed problems of communication. It comprised more than a dozen elementary and nursery schools scattered several miles apart. Worse, the reputation of the schools was not very encouraging. There were rumors of conflicts between the teachers, a lack of facilities for the team, an authoritarian director, difficult parents. These rumors and the rather vague structure of the school district persuaded the psychologist to seek our advice.

FOUR PRELIMINARY STEPS

As a first step, the group sought an approach strategy that would, *from the outset,* be based on a clear definition of the relationship between the team and the teachers, and hence establish a functional context for their work. The team felt that several practical suggestions set out in our book *Il Mago Smagato (The Magician Without Magic)* were of fundamental importance:

- Respect the existing hierarchy in all dealings with the school system.

- Avoid giving a negative connotation to particular individuals or to the school system as a whole.

- Adopt an unambiguous position, but without condescending.

The psychologist realized that his first task was to ignore the web of rumors surrounding the school district, in order to protect his own freedom to maneuver. After several hours of discussion, the team defined a strategy for dealing with what seemed a particularly delicate situation. It involved four stages, all characteristic of the systemic approach:

- The team's first contacts with the director.

- The team's first formal meeting with the director.

- The psychologist's meeting with the chairman of the parents' association.

- The team's initial observations.

The team's first contacts with the director

The team's first approach to the school district was through the director. That approach was particularly important because it was their only opportunity to convey several clear relational messages to the system:

- The team was answerable to the city government, not to the director of the local school district.

- The team was part of a center whose task was to coordinate school health regulations throughout the metropolitan area.

- Although the team was working within the school district, it must not be considered part of it.

■ The team was a link between the city government and the schools.

How could we ensure that these messages would be clearly understood?

Having rejected the idea of an explicit verbal statement as risky and unproductive, the team settled on an indirect (implicit) method: a letter of introduction. In fact, the letter simply restated the positive response of the city government to the district's request for a team of psychologists.

The letter of introduction was thus an official act by which the city presented the team as "its own." By that act the city informed the director that the team owed allegiance to an external authority, not to the school district. We insisted on such a letter —not to set the team up in a privileged position (which would have been counterproductive), but to assure them a degree of freedom and autonomy in the school district. The letter also gave the team its first chance to open the channels of communication between the city, the school district, and the research team.

An important fact mentioned in the letter was the number of hours both members of the team would have to devote to the school district. It was all the more reassuring to the potential clients, in view of the district's poor experiences with peripatetic experts; and it was not open to discussion inasmuch as the school district was simply asked to take note of it. The hours were, in fact, laid down in the agreement between the team and the city government.

The team meets the director

The director of a school district wields the highest authority in the schools, and anyone joining the establishment must, of course, report to him first. In the case under review such a meeting seemed doubly essential in view of the fact that the director was rumored to be an unbending authoritarian, but very efficient. The team found it difficult to determine whether his being something of a political personality influenced such judgments. The team could not ignore the director's political affiliation, since it might well interfere in communications between the city, the team, and the school district. To contact members of his staff and bypass him would have been to snub him. The director would of course define the relationship between the team and the staff as a coalition against him, with easily imagined consequences.[1]

The telephone call.   The psychologist, once he could be reasonably certain that the letter of introduction had arrived, called the director to suggest a meeting. That conversation was a matter of some importance: it was the first concrete exchange of messages, and it could make or break all subsequent relationships. Nor was it by chance that the psychologist (not the therapist) made the call; that choice had a precise communicational function. As the head of the team of psychologists, he was calling the head of the school district, thus acknowledging the director as the person in charge. The tone of his telephone call was bound to have a bearing on the team's relationship with the director; it, too, had been the subject of prior group discussion.

In the call, the psychologist announced himself as the person mentioned in the letter from the city. He was here confronted with the first of several unforeseen circumstances: the letter had not yet arrived. He explained that the letter of introduction was in the mail, and proposed a meeting in order for the team to learn about the general situation of the schools and what they expected from the team; perhaps the director would have valuable suggestions about how to meet those expectations. The psychologist's nondeclared objective was to "metacommunicate" his personal respect for the director, and the wish to collaborate with him. The director replied in a cordial but condescending tone: he would be happy to meet them, but in view of his many duties it was difficult to find time at short notice. To emphasize that point, he read out some of his important appointments during the next few days. After a pause, he suggested several possible dates. The psychologist said that he appreciated the problem, but gave two different dates as the only ones during which the team would be free in the near future. The director, though clearly put out, agreed to one of these two dates and the telephone conversation came to an end. On first impression, the director seemed more accommodating than the team had been given to expect.

The meeting.   A few days later the psychologist and the psychomotor therapist called on the director in person. On their arrival, the director cut short his conversation with a group of teachers and welcomed them cordially. He was a tall, well-built man with a barely perceptible smile and a self-assured expression. He remarked that his office was not available and invited both to sit down at the desks of an empty classroom—"The most important thing is to get this over with quickly, because there's so much to do" seemed to be his first implicit message. He went on to express his satisfaction at having a permanent team with a fixed number of hours at long last; the other teams had just appeared on the scene, made a few comments, and vanished, leaving everything as it was, if not worse. He then added with emphasis: "This weekly schedule set out in your letter of introduction must be scrupulously adhered to, just like the school schedule." Next, he described the various schools in the district, meticulously listing the number of classes, of teachers, and above all of handicapped or "difficult" children in each one. Finally, he invited the team to his office, where, having sat down behind his desk, he returned to the long sequence of difficult situations waiting for the team. The psychologist expressed his astonishment at the scope of these problems. He asked the director how they could best, most systematically, come to grips with so vast an establishment. He posed the problem as a choice between irregular excursions into the various associated schools, or systematic involvement in just a few of them. The director expressed his preference for limited intervention, in keeping with the limited availability of the team. The psychologist welcomed this choice, but remarked that the final decision rested with the city and the department that posted him to the school district. The director appeared annoyed with this implicit definition of the relationship. During the moment of tension that followed, the psychologist realized how risky but indispensable his move had been. To set implicit limits on the director's authority was an essential step in defining their relationship. The psychologist averted the threat of competition by assuring the director that his preference would most likely be respected. He added that after the matter was settled, the team would submit a precise schedule to him. This sufficed to relieve tensions and restore agreement on many problems mentioned by the director, and particularly those involving handicapped children.

The situation of these children posed a further delicate communication challenge. The psychologist felt strongly that the problem lay not with their handicaps, but with the programs designed to deal with them. The psychologist wanted the director to adopt the systemic approach, an approach that ran counter to his expressed views.

Accordingly the psychologist stressed that the team would direct all its energies to the problems created by the presence of handicapped children, but that to do so effectively, the entire school system would have to be involved. It would not be possible to help the handicapped children without studying their total context.[2] He added that, as a consequence, the team would have to participate, though sporadically, in the activities of the entire school district.

The director, who had been listening with a frown, suddenly vented his misgivings. "How?" he demanded. The psychologist explained that the team had no intention of interfering in matters that didn't concern them; they only wanted to render the most effective assistance possible to pupils in difficulty. However, concentrating only on the handicapped children would prove counterproductive—like other children, they could not be truly understood if they were not observed interacting with the whole system of which they were a part. This explanation pacified the director, who, though he looked puzzled, said he quite agreed. He invited the team to meetings of the various school sectors: the staff, the student council, the parents' association, the school board. In short, he embraced the idea that the team should operate in all parts of the system. He thus fell in with the systemic view that no phenomenon can be grasped unless the field of observation includes the whole context in which the phenomenon occurs.

At the end of the discussion, the director arranged a number of meetings to present the team to people connected with some of the schools' departments. That development was a positive result of the discussion because it started communications in a cycle that admirably suited the team: city-team-director-teachers-families-pupils-team.

Problems.   However, some problems remained. There was still a considerable difference between the expectations of the director, who continued to see the problems of the handicapped children in isolation, and the psychologist's systemic approach. The director also had a most unhelpful tendency to rush things: "We must hurry, because there's so much to do," or "Let's drop the preambles and get down to business." Also unhelpful was his habit of laying down the law about the structure of meetings: "Let's sit in a classroom," or "Let's go into the office."

The team didn't know what to make of the director's insistence that they adhere to a rigid schedule from the outset. Was this a wish to collaborate closely with the team, or was it an implicit declaration of a wish to control? While no one would have questioned the director's right to exercise control, even over the work of the team, the team felt it must resist every attempt to define the relationship in authoritarian rather than cooperative terms, or to rob it of the autonomy it enjoyed thanks to its external affiliations. In what way and to what extent could the director then be allowed to have a say over the activity of these outside experts? In what capacity was he entitled to intervene in the work of specialists operating in a wider framework? Clearly, this problem involved the very presence of the team in the school district, and the solution was neither to retreat from the district nor to submit completely to it, but once again to establish a collaborative relationship with the director and the staff. That relationship would rest on the solution of the problems bedeviling the schools, but it required the prior definition of the relationship between the team and the schools. And this would have to be resolved by appropriate forms of behavior.

Discussion with the chairman of the school board. Much as it was thought advisable to approach the teachers through the director, so it was best to approach the parents through their representative. Elected directly by the parents, the chairman of the school board played an important role in the school system.[3] The team's objectives were:

- To define the relationship between the team and the parents.

- To observe the relationship between the parents and the schools.

- To propose direct collaboration between the team and the parents.

The telephone call and the definition of the relationship. In this case, too, the psychologist telephoned the chairman and invited him to a meeting, having first informed the director in order to avoid all misunderstandings. The telephone call to the chairman had the implicit aim of establishing a precise definition of the relationship between the team and the parents. The parents should consider the team not as part of the school system, nor as completely outside it, but as something simultaneously in and out. The team wished to define its relationship with the parents as one of autonomous collaboration partly detached from the dynamics of the schools. The psychologist therefore telephoned from the city offices and not from one of the schools and suggested a meeting in the City Hall. At the same time, he introduced himself as the representative of the team that would be working in the schools. He did not have to state explicitly that they were both inside and outside the school system, since he defined the relationship implicitly and very effectively by arranging the meeting at City Hall.

The discussion. The chairman of the school board, a man of about forty, seemed nervous when he presented himself at City Hall. Sitting down across from him, the psychologist again stated the purpose of the meeting, which was for the team to learn what the parents expected. The chairman promptly replied that the most important thing was "to help the handicapped children. That is the real problem." He added that several remedies had been tried in the past but with poor results. The psychologist responded that, in his view, the problem of these children would remain unsolved unless it was treated in a much wider context.

He asserted that the best way of helping handicapped children was not by treating them as special cases but by making their communications with everyone around them as functional as possible. He proposed that the team should be allowed to attend school board meetings to learn more about the problems of handicapped children. The response was most positive. The chairman agreed emphatically, suggesting that a special rule authorizing such participation be written into the constitution. The psychologist stressed the importance of close collaboration between the team and the parents, and added that he was always available should parents wish him to probe more deeply into problems concerning their relationship with their children. The chairman seemed interested, but remarked that since his term of office would be over in a few months, he would be unable to contribute as much as he would have liked.

The handicapped son.   The chairman suddenly shifted the discussion to personal matters. His smile disappeared and his voice choked as he told the psychologist that he was the father of a severely handicapped child. "My son," he said, "has completely changed my home life." He had made every conceivable sacrifice to cure the child, but to no avail. At school the boy made no progress, but this was partly because he had been unable to find a teacher who "really accepted him."

And then there was the attitude of some parents. The chairman confided that a major obstacle to the enrollment of these "sick" children was that some parents considered their presence prejudicial to the welfare of their own, "normal" children. The director was doing his best, but some situations were very difficult to change.

The psychologist said that he fully understood and added that he considered the chairman's collaboration extremely important to the team. But the chairman seemed discouraged and the discussion ended with vague references to a possible collaboration in the future.

Reflections and hypotheses

This discussion helped the team to understand the context in which it had to work:

- The chairman of the school board had a gravely handicapped child.

- The director was regarded as a serious and efficient person.

- The chairman's handicapped son made little progress at school because of the incompetence of his teachers.

- The parents were divided into two parties: those who approved of admitting handicapped children into "normal" classes and those who did not.

The chairman had made no reference to the nonteaching staff, even though they often have a very special and delicate relationship with handicapped children (for instance, when the children need help with bodily functions).

Now the psychologist could frame the following working hypotheses:

- Since the director had mentioned that he hoped the team could solve the problem of the handicapped children, and since it later appeared that the chairman of the school board was the father of one, the request for the dispatch of a team of psychologists must have come from the chairman himself.

- The fact that the chairman had had problems with his handicapped child was responsible for the school district's marked concentration on the problem of handicapped children, and was a cause of the rift between families for and against the admission of handicapped children, the latter opposed to the chairman. That opposition was, however, carefully masked because it could not be stated openly in the presence of the father of a handicapped child.[4]

In what follows, testing the truth of these hypotheses will help us to examine the implementation of the team's overall operational plan.

The initial phase

For the first month or so, the team spent most of its time meeting the various subgroups of the school district, in order to observe their working context. They considered this the natural extension of the original contact procedures. The main objective was, again, to formulate a program meeting the real needs of the schools. The team also wanted to make sure that their introduction into the schools allowed relations with the teachers and parents to follow the pattern set in meetings with the director and the chairman. And they wanted to observe the relational context in order to verify our hypotheses and gain a better understanding of the special phenomena they would be encountering.

First, the director presented the team to the staff of one of the schools, as part of their original agreement. It should be added that the city government and the office the psychologists worked for had meanwhile communicated their decision to the director: the team would work in just three of the schools in the district, all relatively close to the city center. This greatly eased the task of the team, even during the initial phase.

THE SCHOOLS

The First School

The school district had a number of schools, one of which housed the administrative offices. This part of the establishment seemed to have few problems other than minor differences between the teachers and some of the parents or pupils. For the rest, nearly the entire staff, from teachers to custodians, seemed rather under the director's thumb, although they would show occasional signs of opposition to his "arbitrary" rulings.

Toward the psychologist, the staff seemed cautious, even if their verbal expressions indicated appreciation and esteem. Their attitude to the psychomotor therapist, however, showed that they considered her more as a "teacher's helper" than a specialist in rehabilitation.

The psychologist's office. The first tangible problem was finding an office for the psychologist. There was the usual lack of space, and the administrative department was in an old building that had long since become inadequate for the growing school population. But the psychologist thought it essential to have a private office—not only for conducting meetings, but also as a concrete sign of his presence in the school; without a place of his own, he was bound to be considered a nebulous figure. A permanent office thus served as a message that the psychologist existed and was at everyone's disposal, a sign that changes were taking place. *Territory,* much like *time,* is an important variable in the organization of inter-actions.

The psychologist accordingly impressed upon the director that an office was essential for him to do his work effectively. The director decried the lack of office space; plainly he was merely trying to put the psychologist off. When the latter replied that he knew of an office that could readily be adapted to his needs, the director claimed it was already earmarked for another activity. The psychologist calmly repeated that he would be unable to do his job without an office. Within a few days, the director came around to his point of view.

With this minor exception, there was little friction. The staff at the first school had a number of expectations for the research team, which could be summed up under two headings:

- To conduct refresher courses for teachers.

- To solve interpersonal problems.

The second school

In the second school there was such tension between the teachers that they were never able to agree on any practical steps. A group of older teachers were opposed to a small group of young ones, who considered the first group too individualistic, unwilling to work for the common good. Yet a third group wished to appear independent and impartial, and sided with neither group. Finally, there were a few teachers who, considering themselves the permanent targets of criticism by all the rest, preferred to act alone and almost in secret. All these divisions were, however, kept in check: a veil had been drawn over them as an acknowledgment that no one wanted to engage in open warfare.

When the team arrived, the first move by the teachers was to draw the veil even tighter. The team was obviously welcome and could do what it liked, as long as it did not question the relationship between the teachers. Moreover, as this second school was far away from the first, the team was treated as an emissary of the director. This explained why some teachers acted defiantly, while others were formal and respectful. As a result, the team was frozen out, which hampered its effectiveness. The teachers did approach the team with problems, but just the usual cases of pupils in difficulties. The teachers considered the idea of joining working groups an utter waste of time.

The parents sensed the deep division among the teachers and showed their resentment by rarely attending school meetings, thus in a sense washing their hands of responsibility for their children's education.

The children, too, felt these undercurrents. The most apparent effect on them was to make them very dependent on their individual teacher.

How should the team behave in this situation? Should it simply resign itself and not disturb the harmful and precarious equilibrium, or was it essential to lift the veil that immobilized the teachers' interpersonal dynamics? The team decided to proceed slowly. To begin with, it would try to fulfill the teachers' immediate expectations. Later it would try to create new expectations, and thus alter the teachers' interpersonal dynamics.

The nursery school

The third school where the team was to work was the nursery school. Here, having explained the school's problems to the team, the director presented them to the staff. The problems, he said, were:

- Besides a capable young teacher whom he had put in charge, the nursery school had two new teachers whose attitude was causing concern, and some part-timers.

- The general situation of the nursery school was unusually problematical.

- His other responsibilities prevented him from dealing with the situation.

The team inferred that the director was trying to shift the responsibility for dealing with this difficult situation onto their shoulders.

During their contacts with the staff, the team discovered that the situation was extremely confused and getting worse. First of all, there were two nursery schools in the building—one public and the other private. The two schools operated in separate (though adjacent) classrooms, but shared a large playground and a common lunchroom and kitchen. The teachers in the two schools, moreover, were differentiated administratively, both by contract and by salary. Leaving aside for the moment the problem of the proximity of a private school in which it was not clear whether the team was to operate, the most difficult point seemed to be the condition of the staff. The public school had two sections, staffed by four teachers in all, plus a nonteaching assistant and a cook. It was expected that three or four more teachers would be added, transferred from a center for motor-impaired children, although they would be answerable to the central school district. They would in fact arrive if a tentative plan to admit handicapped children to the school was carried out.

The question of the admission of handicapped children to both nursery schools was the first and most important cause of alliances and clear-cut antagonisms. The team watched these developments at close quarters. The private school wanted nothing to do with the handicapped children. In the public school, even though there was little likelihood of a policy adopted by the director being rejected, the head teacher and one of the young part-time teachers became his staunch supporters. By contrast, the recently hired teachers, two middle-aged single women who lived together, quickly distanced themselves from an experiment they considered futile. As a result, two distinct and hostile groups, the young and the old, quickly crystallized. A third group, those who had meanwhile come from the center for motor-impaired children, at first joined forces with the younger staff, but later tried to adopt a neutral stance in what had rapidly turned into a cold war, a "symmetrical escalation" with no remission.

The opposing groups engaged in crude personal attacks on each other in order to justify their present hostility. There were murmurs about "those dirty old bags" who had been kicked out of several schools because of incompetence, and sarcastic references to the head teacher's inexperience and her problems with her fiancé.

The children's mothers were of course upset by stories the head teacher fed to them "in confidence" to convince them of the backwardness of the two "old crones." Thus the head teacher used her position to escalate the cold war, and her opponents reacted in kind. The children had become mere pawns in the war. A great fuss was made over the handicapped children whenever "the other side" was watching, but very little serious effort to integrate them into the activities of the school. The children were asked to sing, to play, and to work, they were shown films, but everything was done in a ferociously competitive atmosphere. The two older teachers, who seemed to be losing the battle, ended up barricading themselves in their classroom and forbidding all their pupils to go into the head teacher's room—even those whom she had taught the year before.

It seemed incredible that so wide a gulf should have opened up in so short a time, not only between the teachers but also between the parents.

The team did not have to wait long for attempts to draw it into coalitions. The psychologist soon became an object of attention and confidence by the head teacher, who missed no opportunity to deride the "old girls." These two first believed that the team were conspiring against them with the younger staff, and with the director's blessing. But they soon learned better, after the team exhibited an attitude that left no one in doubt about their neutrality. Toward this end they took the following steps:

- In his discussions with the young head teacher, the psychologist made it plain that anything likely to improve the school's functional dynamics would enjoy his full support. But he discouraged attempts to run down "the others," making it clear by his behavior that he was not about to take sides.

- The psychologist visited the two older teachers in their own classroom, showing approval of their work and acknowledging their long experience.

- In his dealings with the head teacher as well as with the two older teachers, the psychologist directed attention away from the interpersonal problems, and towards common objectives.

- He entered into a collaboration with the teachers of the motor-impaired children, making sure that this relationship could not be mistaken for a coalition against any other parties.

- He tactfully informed the director of the consequences of his blind support for the head teacher, and pointed to the need for his personal attention in this delicate situation.

It gradually became clear that the staff—already weary of their exhausting battles—were anxious to collaborate with the team, and expected it to solve their interpersonal problems (though each faction secretly continued to hope that it could use the team as a lever against the others). The team itself felt quite optimistic about its role at this point.

THE OVERALL OPERATIONAL PLAN

Having completed the initial observations, the team now prepared to tackle a triple task:

- To analyze the organization of the interactions in the three schools.

- To compare the expectations of the teaching staff, the pupils, and the parents with the actual operational capabilities of the team.

- To choose operational methods best suited to dealing with the problems of each particular school.

The choice of operational methods

The team knew that the choice of a concrete approach to fitting itself into the context of the school system was crucial to its hope for results. It was most anxious to avoid the mistake of resorting to "prefabricated recipes," of making automatic use of standard methods. The team therefore based its operational methods on hypotheses derived from its analysis of the three schools. Its methods of intervention focused attention on the starting positions of the various parties and members of the staff. To that end, the team decided:

- To hold regular weekly meetings with the director in order to monitor its relationship with him over time.

- To attend occasional staff and parents meetings (but only upon the director's express invitation) in order to exert a positive influence on the interactions within the school system.

- To organize a teachers' group on the "verbal method of communication" as a means of overcoming interpersonal difficulties.

- To set up teachers' and parents' groups to discuss "analogic communication" as a potential cure of current conflicts.

- To meet with teachers and the parents of pupils with problems (when explicitly requested) to improve communication and gather information about needed intervention.

- To be available for individual interviews based on the systemic approach.

As the reader will see, some of these methods applied in certain schools, and some in others, depending on their requirements.

Presenting the program to the teachers

It would have been a great mistake for the team to impose its program on the schools. In particular, failing to present its proposals as anything more than "working hypotheses" for the teachers' inspection, and to gain their support and collaboration, would have been provocative and perhaps even paralyzing: the team would have indicated that it was interested only in one-way communication. Such mistakes invariably elicit negative responses. In our case, the teachers would have rejected the operational plan, as well as the team itself, in response to the implicit message that the team didn't need their help.

before applying the plan, therefore, the team, with the agreement of the director, presented it formally to the teachers. They raised no serious objections, but the director made a few adverse comments—not about the program as such but about the theory underlying it. In fact, his remarks were intended to show that he was still the "boss," and hence to counterbalance the privileged position the team enjoyed. As he did not, however, question the substance of the program, the team was careful not to slide into useless disputes about theory, but adopted what might be called a "metacomplementary" attitude: by acknowledging his observations it endorsed his role as "chief," that endorsement being a functional part of the implementation of the program. At the same time, the team communicated its indifference to questions of power and control to the teaching staff: all that mattered was constructive collaboration. In that way the team was able to establish a good working relationship with the staff.

IMPLEMENTING THE PLAN

The presentation of its working plan helped to clarify the team's position and enabled it to steer a clear course during the entire school year. Naturally, there were unforeseen circumstances, and the team also made several mistakes. They fared differently in each of the schools. We can say without hesitation that the team made a considerable contribution to the forging of ties between the various parties involved, helping to improve communications in all the schools, and in no case making things worse. This conclusion is based on a careful analysis of the work done and of the views of the teaching staff, and thus bears witness to the validity of the strategy used.

Meetings with the director

The office assigned to the psychologist was on the floor above the director's office. When the meetings between them were reviewed at the end of the year, it appeared that they met in the psychologist's office as often as in the director's. Still, the director left no one in any doubt that he was in charge of the entire school district and of all that happened in it. He jealously guarded his position, reacting strongly against anything that might in any way weaken it. It would certainly have been impossible to have a single productive meeting with him had the psychologist appeared as a competitor. That is why all the psychologist's messages to him were designed to signal that there was no question of competition in their relationship. He did this by

- Explicitly acknowledging and respecting the director's role.

- Keeping all communications at the level of productive collaboration.

- Sending the director the same messages of "confirmation" and collaboration through the other groups in the school.

- Acknowledging the director's heavy responsibility for everything that happened in the school (trying nevertheless to portray the director implicitly as a "victim" of his own dominant role, so as to curb certain excesses on his part).

When it finally became possible to go beyond defining the relationship and the need for the director to be "in control," he turned out to be a most affable, understanding, and efficient person. But it wasn't easy to reach that stage: the team had run the risk of being mistaken for rivals, and, conversely, of sinking to slavish complementarity. There were some particularly difficult moments, as witness the following

Coping with a symmetrical escalation. At the very beginning of the team's activity in the schools, the psychomotor therapist made the mistake of not adhering strictly to her schedule, and the director's reaction was strong.

Even earlier, he had shown an ambiguous attitude toward the therapist, and she had responded impulsively with a symmetrical attitude, reaffirming her position as a "municipal employee" and underscoring her professional status. This breakdown in communication quickly led to a complete rupture between the therapist and the director.

The director responded to her expressions of opposition by drawing up another rigid schedule and by treating her in all respects as if she were a substitute teacher.

The psychologist realized that the director's unusually severe treatment of the therapist, subsequently banishing her to the schools far away from the director's office, was intended to split the team and to communicate the director's objections to the psychomotor therapist's apparent alliance with the psychologist. He had a legitimate reason for moving her from the administrative offices, though, since another psychomotor therapist had just arrived to work part-time on a different project.

The psychologist did not mention the subject to the director except briefly at a weekly meeting, when he let it appear that he understood and shared the director's apprehensions.

Towards the psychomotor therapist, who was clearly passing through a depressive phase, he adopted a supportive attitude, analyzing the interpersonal situation and redefining the objectives to be reached. Realizing that it was impossible to restore functional communication between the two quickly, the psychologist saw his immediate task as saving the unity of the team, and maintaining functional contacts with the director.

He reached these objectives by two stages. He first of all expressed his acceptance of the director's right to have the final say, something the psychomotor therapist had refused to do. The psychologist used various occasions to adopt an attitude complementary to the director's. The next tactic was more complicated: he suggested a course of lectures on the psychomotor education of preschool children (highly topical because of the newly arrived motor-impaired children). His suggestion was greeted with enthusiasm by all the nursery-school teachers, who commended it warmly to the director.

Now, that course could be given only by the psychomotor therapist, so that by sanctioning the lectures, the director implicitly recognized her professional standing. The therapist, meanwhile, implicitly recognized the director's authority, since the course could not be given without his express agreement. Thus a serious rift that had threatened the operational efficiency of the team was averted.

The danger of becoming a mere ornament. Relations with the director were also in danger of deteriorating into a repetitive mechanism of the complementary type, in which the team would be rigidly cast as the director's puppet. That would mean forfeiting its credibility and autonomy to become a mere feather in the director's cap—"his" team. That would simply have strengthened the homeostatic tendencies of the system, reinforcing the prevailing interaction pattern.

Verbal declarations might well have given rise to symmetrical responses that would have served no purpose. The psychologist accordingly decided once more to resort to behavioral messages—small, apparently trivial gestures which nevertheless signaled unequivocally that the team was autonomous and independent.

For example, after a lecture to the staff, the director, who had taken the chair, invited the speaker, sitting on his right, and the psychologist, on his left, to have a drink with him. Nothing more natural, you might think. But the psychologist, weighing the context, realized that by going with the director and turning his back on the teachers, he would have signaled publicly that he was about to play a role strictly complementary to the director's. He therefore politely declined the invitation.

We have already mentioned that the psychologist and the director did not invariably meet in the latter's office. This was the result of a deliberate policy. The psychologist felt that the act of "going downstairs" or "going upstairs" was a communication, and hence did not hesitate to go down to the director whenever he felt the need to minimize, by means of complementary behavior, the risk of a symmetrical escalation. On the other hand, the psychologist would wait for the director to come up to his office whenever there was the slightest threat of his role becoming too complementary.

During their meetings, the psychologist tried to eliminate all traces of rigidity in the definition of their relationship. He kept a tight check on the relational aspects of their communication, with a view to demonstrating, in their verbal contact, his complete independence of mind. In the relational context, however, he adopted postures, gestures, a tone of voice, to signal that his position was complementary to the director's.

Ultimately the many meetings proved to be occasions for fruitful collaboration. The situation, which had at first fluctuated painfully, eventually settled on a level of reciprocal communication. Towards the end of the team's mission in the school district, the problem of the definition of the relationship dissolved, and the parties were able to collaborate peacefully on their objectives.

Staff meetings

Of the various school activities, the staff meetings were undoubtedly of particular importance.

A case of musical chairs. An interesting example of analogic communication can be observed in the "mysterious" case of the psychologist's chair. The chair was moved from place to place at successive staff meetings: from the director's table it was moved to a position between him and the teachers.

At the first staff meeting, the team had been invited to sit at the director's right, facing the room full of teachers. The result was the creation of two distinct factions, divided not only by their placement but by the table acting as a palisade between them. Most of the teachers were seated according to school, and communication between groups did not seem to be particularly free. Some teachers were obviously ill at ease, some felt that they were being ignored, and others seemed intolerant or aggressive. But this is not surprising, since staff meetings were rare occasions for teachers from the entire school district to come together.

The team, facing them from behind the director's table, was bound to seem part of the "management" side. For that reason, the psychologist made it known, without putting it into words, that this seating arrangement did not suit him: at later meetings his chair gradually moved from the director's side, except on occasions of particular importance. The psychologist preferred to sit at an equal distance from both parties, as he did at most meetings. His equidistance was a pointed analogic communication that prevented the teachers from seeing him as the director's stooge or ally.

The psychologist's blunder. At staff meetings, it was possible to detect a vast range of interpersonal attitudes. Some of these were reflected in the structure of the institution, namely:

- The general attitude of teachers to the director.

- The relationships between individual teachers.

- The teachers' attitude toward staff in other schools in the district.

- The teachers' and the director's attitude toward the team.

All these relationships and attitudes were of interest to the team, since they illuminated certain events in the schools.

The team's participation in school meetings, however, entailed risks. The team's presence might be taken as a form of meddling in matters beyond its field of expertise. Also, such meetings could become occasions for attempts to draw the team into alliances, thus undermining its determination to show that it was nonpartisan and not part of the school system.

Despite these good intentions, the psychologist committed a grave error during a meeting devoted to a recently introduced grading system. The teachers had made an effort to fall in with the new system, but many of them were uncomfortable with a few innovations that seemed hard to understand or to implement. Some teachers, in fact, continued to use the old marking system on the new report cards.

During the discussion, the psychologist picked up one such report and pointed out the mistakes. This was read as a double message by the teachers: that he was adopting a superior attitude, and that he rejected the views of the teachers opposed to the new report system (thereby forming a coalition with the director, who was present). The teachers' response was immediate; this was one of the rare occasions on which they took a united defensive stand. It should be noted that although the teacher whose report was criticized had not been present, that didn't change the significance of this mistaken intervention. As a result, the relationship between the psychologist and the teachers was threatened. To repair it, the psychologist sent a host of verbal and nonverbal messages of esteem and appreciation, as well as appeals for help and collaboration in a number of delicate situations.[5]

Behavioral messages. Observing relationships was not, of course, the sole reason the team attended teachers' meetings. Observation as an end in itself would have been pointless. The team's objective was to intervene by nonverbal messages, coupled with appropriate attitudes and actions, and hence to produce a salutary effect. Examples of such behavior were:

- Listening attentively to all proposals and stressing their positive aspects.

- Offering verbal comments only when asked for.

- Adopting a complementary attitude whenever a symmetrical escalation was about to take place (in other words, being cooperative to fend off competitive behavior).

- Expressing puzzlement and uncertainty in the face of problems posed for the sole purpose of defining relationships.

- Avoiding all attempts to defend one party against the other, but adopting a detached attitude at times of conflict while supporting attempts to solve problems or to reach concrete objectives.

In the cases of the admission of handicapped children and the new grading system, every teacher had his own views, and the purpose of the discussion was to examine them all and arrive at an acceptable solution. Unfortunately, it often happens in conflicts that opinions are put forward merely to express animosities, thus obscuring the business at hand.

On such occasions the presence of the team proved very useful in restoring functional communication by means of the pragmatic messages we have described. While it was impossible to determine the precise effect of such messages, it was often possible to detect the expected responses both in attitudes and in actions.

The school board

The school board, in which all the district's schools were represented, provided the team with a rare occasion for observing the relationships between the various components of the system. Because this body had a powerful voice in important aspects of school life (such as selection of textbooks, arrangement of classes, allocation of funds), it could help solve problems affecting the entire school district.

As we saw, the psychologist agreed at the start with the director and the chairman of the school board that the team should attend these meetings. Unfortunately, the psychologist's schedule prevented him from attending more than a few times; and although he thus could not draw clear conclusions, he was able to observe several interesting phenomena.

First of all, at these meetings, too, there was a polar seating scheme: on the one side sat the chairman, with the director sitting on his right, and on the other side were the teachers and parents. (Curiously, these meetings were the only official occasions when a representative of the nursery school could communicate with representatives of the primary schools—an indication of how important the board was in organizing interactions throughout the district.) The relationship between the various representatives seemed to be cautious. Predictably, the director tried to lead the meeting, with the chairman weakly disputing his authority. When calling on speakers to address the meeting, or cutting them off, he habitually added that he was the elected chairman. The psychologist's attendance seemed to be greatly appreciated. Many of those present turned to him for information or advice on various problems—especially on one that was pressing: how to deal with a large influx of pupils from other schools. The meeting was glad to take the psychologist's advice to concentrate on the needs of the new pupils.

The metacommunication group

In the first school, which housed the offices of the director and school secretary, the teachers looked to the team to improve the relational dynamics between teachers, pupils, and parents. The team proposed creating a group to study "metacommunication"—communication about communication. The aim of the new group was to analyze the relationships involved in (not the contents of) communications between pupils, teachers, and parents. The intention was to improve the ability of every member of the metacommunications group to describe his current relationships with persons outside the group. The psychologist focused on a severe case of communications failure (which was presented by one of the members) and invited the group to define what aspects of the relationship were likely to aggravate matters and to propose methods for rendering communication more functional. Nearly all the teachers in the first school—but none of the others—agreed to hold weekly meetings. These were attended by ten or twelve teachers.

The group had many ups and downs, and in midyear the psychologist decided to disband it. What had gone wrong? To begin with, the group had created a privileged relationship between some teachers and the psychologist from which the director was excluded, thus opposing his determination to run all school activities. Not surprisingly, therefore, he treated the group with suspicion. While displaying interest and goodwill on the verbal level, he did what he could to thwart the group on the practical level. In particular, although the group had been set up for professional training purposes, the director forced it to meet outside the twenty hours a month provided by law for teachers' refresher courses. Ultimately he introduced his own refresher course, and asked the participants, who included some members of the group, to devote all their training time to it.

While he may not have been deliberately trying to impede

the work of the group, he did in fact cause great difficulties. There was, moreover, the grave danger that the group might lead to a competitive relationship between the director and the psychologist. Thus the director might interpret the teachers' praise of the psychologist's skill as a challenge to his own authority. The psychologist, finally, interested in improving the relationship between the teachers, pupils, and parents, could not forget that the quality of such relationships was inseparable from the quality of his relationship (and that of other members of the school) with the director.

Breaking a repetitive symmetrical cycle.　In every classroom there are difficult relational situations. Often the teacher does not know what to do with unstable, irresolute, withdrawn, or dependent pupils, or with parents who disparage their children in front of classmates or spring to their defense by discrediting their teachers. Remaining in control of the relationship in such circumstances means being able to metacommunicate about the situation and to act in a way that takes account of all its problems.

During the group's third meeting, the discussion turned to a particularly difficult pupil. Stephen, a disturbed nine-year-old, kept running between classrooms, rifling his comrades' satchels, and fighting with the other boys, one in particular. Towards the girls he behaved quite differently, kissing, hugging, and squeezing them. When reprimanded by the teacher, he said nothing but would soon start all over again. He refused to do any schoolwork unless threatened with punishment. His teacher was exasperated at having to use authoritarian methods, which she heartily disliked. She had several discussions with Stephen's mother, who supplied some important background information. Stephen's family was very poor and uneducated. His father, a thirty-two-year-old asthmatic, drew a disability allowance; his mother, twenty-seven, worked as a domestic servant. Stephen's grandmother, who lived with the family, looked after him and his older brother; unlike the parents, she was permissive and protective. His mother was expecting a third child, apparently had a lover, and was continually fighting with her husband. Their apartment was old, small, and unhealthy. For a long time, Stephen had lived with an uncle who eventually died of cirrhosis of the liver. When Stephen came back home, he and his brother started stealing bicycle wheels and other things. "When I took him to a psychiatrist, I was told to smack his hands," the mother said.

Hearing this account, the group realized that Stephen's background was full of symmetrical oppositions: grandmother against parents, parents against each other, Stephen against his brother (even though they stole together). The family was poorer than their neighbors, which made it hard for Stephen to make friends with children his age. The group felt that Stephen tended to reproduce in class the symmetrical relational experiences of his home, and that he expected reactions like those he got at home. His relationship with his teacher, however, alternated between symmetry and complementarity. Why? The group framed the hypothesis that here he reproduced *two types* of relationships: one associated with his (permissive) grandmother, another with his (authoritarian) parents. And, in fact, when the teacher's reaction was like his parents', it got results; other relational models were ineffective.

The team then suggested that in her nonverbal communications with Stephen she should convey trust and understanding by warm and attentive behavior, while verbally insisting that Stephen obey the school rules. By thus associating the relational model of Stephen and his grandmother with that of Stephen and his parents, the group hoped not only to break the repetitive cycle of symmetrical responses but also to improve Stephen's learning ability.

This approach helped the teacher escape from an impasse and allowed her to act with much greater assurance. These changes were bound to affect Stephen, who gradually improved his behavior and work in class, even though he still had relational difficulties.

The analysis of metacommunication also improved the teachers' relationships with handicapped children: sometimes merely changing their way of looking at their own communications was enough to cause other changes.

Disbanding the group.　After the group had been active for about two months, the center that had originally assigned the psychologist to the school decided to run outside refresher courses for teachers. The idea was to free them from the constraints of their work, and to give them a different set of experiences.

The director declared himself opposed to moving the metacommunications group to the new location assigned by the center, and he resumed his old tactic of sabotaging the group. *This was the crucial point in the psychologist's relationship with him.* It would have been quite natural to treat the director's actions as authoritarian and provocative behavior and to slip into a vicious symmetrical cycle. Instead, the psychologist, supported by our research team, realized that the only possible way to progress was to adopt a complementary attitude.

To that end, the following strategy was devised. During a meeting of the metacommunications group, the psychologist told the teachers that he realized that they had been working under pressure and understood why it had occasionally been necessary to postpone meetings. Since the group clearly imposed too great a sacrifice on them, he thought it best to disband it. He did not mention the director's interference.

He added that he was always ready to work with groups on specific projects, if asked. But he wondered whether the rate of dropout from the present group had not indicated waning interest, in which case there would certainly be no demand for new groups. However, if the interest was there, the teachers (not the psychologist) would have to try to remove the obstacles that had stood in the group's way.

This is precisely what happened. The teachers kept asking the director to exempt them from the refresher course so that they could attend groups run by the psychologist. The director eventually gave in, albeit reluctantly. A new group was set up, now to work on specific projects. The first was to study the dynamics of groups and subgroups in classrooms. This project, proposed by the teachers, was intended to smooth the impending restructuring of some of the classes.

The director disliked this arrangement intensely and tried in various ways to win the group back for the refresher course. Despite these difficulties, which threatened a return to a circular relationship, communication between the psychologist, the director, and the teachers remained essentially functional: the group was able to do what it needed to do.

The analogic-communication group

The analogic-communication group differed from the metacommunication group in both aim and method. The aim was no longer the analysis of relational problems at the verbal level; indeed, all verbal references to the relationships between various members were banned. Instead, the group aimed at improving communication between parties at the *nonverbal level*, through a program of active participation. Members of the group were placed in situations requiring them to collaborate on a set goal, which forced them to engage in functional analogic communication (and, consequently, to collaborate to surmount relational difficulties in general).

This group was earmarked for teachers and parents of nursery-school children. We have already observed that, on its arrival at the nursery school, the team encountered a situation so tangled that any attempt to unravel it verbally seemed ill advised. Nor did the analysis of existing relationships hold much promise· symmetrical reactions dominated the whole structure. The solution was to ignore verbal communications between the rival members of the system and to concentrate on changing relationships at the analogic level. The team guessed that if everyone concerned was drawn into a program with a concrete objective, the overall relational situation would improve. Working towards a common goal might cause the members of the parents' and teachers' group to reduce negative feelings, and direct their energies into productive channels. The team would merely act as a catalyst, and with great discretion.

The puppet theater. Puppet theaters hold a great fascination for nursery-school children and provide an excellent educational tool. The private section of the nursery school had a special puppet stage, but it was never used. The psychologist, with the director's consent, suggested to the staff and the parents that they join forces to stage a puppet show. The invitation was extended to teachers and parents in the private school as well as the public one, but the parents in the private section were completely uninterested. Most of the others reacted positively, once they were past their initial surprise.

All they had was the small stage (which was in disrepair); everything else had to be made: the script, the puppets, and the scenery. The psychologist wanted to avoid any too-easy improvisations and the use of ready-made scripts. Everything was to be invented afresh.

Accordingly various groups were formed, each with a specific task. The psychologist made sure that every group included members of the various subgroups, so as to initiate a process of analogic communication. Unfortunately, they could not involve the children directly, though they were of course drawn in as spectators. Their active participation would have interfered with the team's tacit central objective: the improvement of communications between the adults as a prerequisite of a better approach to education.

Almost miraculously, and despite conflicts on both the verbal and the analogic level, the work progressed well. Thus, though rehearsals had to be held evenings and weekends, no one objected. Despite the obstacles, two different plays were produced, one at the middle and the other at the end of the school year.

The work offered many opportunities for close collaboration and laughter. It also gave rise to meetings of great relational interest. One of these meetings lasted a whole day.

A shared weekend. The dress rehearsal demanded the presence of all the members of the various groups. Since that was impossible during school hours, the psychologist suggested a one-day informal get-together over the weekend. The school year was by then drawing to a close and the psychologist thought it was time to test what progress had been made towards the real objective, the improvement of the relational situation. His proposal of a weekend gathering in the nursery school was unanimously approved. After a general meeting attended by the director and the chairman of the parents' association, small working groups were formed. Of these, the group in charge of catering played a particularly important role because it introduced a note of cheerfulness into the relational dynamics.

At the end of the gathering the psychologist made the following observations:

- The group took satisfaction from its achievements.

- There had been quite unexpected collaboration from those teachers who had shown strong opposition to the scheme and who had had problems in their relationships with the other teachers.

- The director, though obviously concerned about his status, had thrown himself wholeheartedly into the work.

- The parents of some pupils had been very generous and helpful.

- The excellent meal, the splendid wine (supplied by the two recently recruited middle-aged women teachers), and the various desserts prepared by the group leader and several mothers had inspired better communication and closer collaboration.

- The playful nature of all the activities and the festive mood made people forget their chronic relational divisions.

On the negative side, the psychologist noted the absence of a teacher who had played a tenacious role in the symmetrical struggle and had now reported sick. There was also some hostility from the regular kitchen and cleaning staff. The team had been wrong in failing to involve the last group more directly. As a reaction, the kitchen staff created difficulties on the pretext that the use of the kitchen by outsiders might upset the normal routine.

All we need add here is that, in addition to the puppet theater, the analogic-communication group also launched schemes to change classroom activities. As a result of these initiatives, old barriers were gradually broken down. Though all relational problems were not, of course, resolved, the analogic-communication group proved to be an effective tool in breaking up the fruitless, repetitive interactions that had squelched all hopes of collaboration.

Teachers and parents request meetings

One of the team's first problems was devising concrete methods for helping children in difficulty. Appeals for such help quickly poured in from teachers and parents, some seeking individual assistance, others general advice. This posed yet another relational problem: no advice could be given until the relational dynamics of the pupil's classroom and family background had been assessed. The team accordingly adopted a two-pronged approach: meeting with the pupil's parents and teachers, and analyzing the flow of communication in the classroom.

The meetings were intended to involve parents and teachers in a systems approach to school activity, and to help them examine their interventions in the child's life against the general background of his relational life. That objective could not always be attained: in some cases the team came up against expectations rigidly opposed to their own; in others they were faced with conflicting expectations of teachers and parents.

The analysis of communications in the classroom was based on:

- Data obtained during the team's meeting with the teacher.

- Observations in the classroom.

- The results of interventions in the classroom at the teacher's explicit request.

The organization of group interactions around a pupil's problems often proved valuable in drawing that pupil into class activities and improving his school performance. Unfortunately, this approach could not be used in the second school, where the handicapped children were used as pawns in a game of symmetrical opposition. Here the psychologist was constantly thwarted and often felt bitter about it, albeit he appeared to carry on as usual. But nothing had really changed. He was simply being used in a relational game, and the rest of the time he was ignored.

Discussions of the systems approach

Part of the psychologist's time was set aside for individual or small-group discussions. These were obviously desired by teachers and parents, but the psychologist felt that, before he acted, he should be asked in writing—such requests would qualify as "cries for help." But how was he to convey this to the parents and teachers? Verbal explanations seemed inappropriate, so he asked the director and the city administration to put a small mailbox near the entrance of each of the three schools. The boxes were reserved strictly for messages to him and conveyed to all concerned the need for written requests. Also, the psychologist's hours were posted beside the boxes.

In practice, the initiative invariably came from teachers who persuaded mothers to take advantage of the psychologist to get to the bottom of their child's behavioral problems. The mother usually sent a request for an interview. A time was then fixed by the psychologist. After a meeting or two with the mother—the father, although invited, was rarely present—the psychologist spoke with the teacher, and finally with the teacher and the parents together. In some cases, the three parties decided to continue with an individual discussion between the pupil and the psychologist. Every session lasted forty-five minutes, but no limit was set to their number. In general, the meetings were continued until the client lost interest or the objective was achieved. The meetings proved to be very important cards in the psychologist's hand. Played well, they could profoundly change the relational dynamics of the school and hence quietly solve previously insoluble problems.

The systemic function of the individual discussions was to correct dysfunctional relationships of long standing, create new relationships, cement good relationships, and guide teachers, pupils, and parents towards solving clearly defined problems.

For instance, one mother, worried by her child's grave learning problems, had written to ask for a meeting with the psychologist. At the first session, she complained that the teacher showed no sympathy for her son. She explained that the child "knew things" at home but kept them to himself at school. The teacher later told the psychologist that this protective mother usually did her son's homework, to make him appear more capable than he was. In short, there was a clash of wills between the teacher and the mother. The pupil was caught in the middle, and hence found it difficult to make progress at school. A series of frank discussions led by the psychologist succeeded in breaking down the antagonism of the two women and finding a satisfactory solution.

However, such meetings can also become a trap for a psychologist. Now he is in the greatest danger of being treated like a doctor, expected to produce infallible prescriptions and immediate cures. The very structure of these meetings helps give him a magical aura.

The only solution is to assign a concrete systemic function to each session. A meeting isn't useful unless it renders systemic communication more functional. To guide people towards a relationship based on trust and collaboration instead of distrust and antipathy is to show them an entirely new way of relating to one another. The results are not always gratifying, and it is not always clear that the solution has been due to the psychologist's intervention. Indeed, it often turns out that the client adopts an attitude that signals the very opposite, as in the following case.

Agreeing to disparage the psychologist.   A mother, alarmed by her son's behavior, applied to the psychologist for help, as did the boy's teacher. The child, about ten years old, repeated certain obsessional gestures—he kept touching his hair, squeezing his legs together, and touching his genitals. Both the mother and the teacher thought he was masturbating, and neither knew how to react. Attempts to make him stop by direct appeals had proved futile. After several meetings with the psychologist, there was a marked improvement in the relationship between the two women, who had previously distrusted each other. But the boy continued his behavior, despite repeated appeals by the two women.

The psychologist—postulating a symmetrical escalation between the two adults (both of whom were sticklers for rules) and the pupil (who asserted his independence through his behavior)—decided to intervene by having the women instruct the boy to persist with his "symptom." The intention was to break the vicious circle by placing the adults in complementary positions towards the pupil, and the pupil in a symmetrical position towards his "symptom." That ploy demanded the collaboration of both women, since both would have to reverse their attitude to the boy. They would have to tell him that they had consulted the psychologist, who had concluded that it was absolutely necessary for the boy to touch himself. The psychologist had decided that the boy must perform his gestures with greater regularity: at intervals of precisely five minutes in class and at home, each day for two weeks.

The women were shocked, but after the psychologist had dispelled their worst fears, they agreed to collaborate. Still, their faces betrayed disbelief.

At the end of the two weeks, the mother admitted that she had not followed instructions, but said that she had nevertheless noticed an improvement in her son, whose compulsion to repeat the offensive gestures seemed to have diminished. The teacher, who had done as instructed, remarked that the boy's behavior seemed to have grown worse, even though—she added, contradicting herself—he now tended to touch himself less often.

During this meeting the psychologist noticed a significant change in the two clients' choice of chairs in his office. While they had sat as far apart as they could during earlier meetings, they now sat close together, near the door. This was their way of communicating analogically their unity in rejecting the psychologist's prescription.

The psychologist realized that he had not managed to win the two women over for his project, and had underestimated their unwillingness to adopt a complementary attitude towards the boy. The consequence was the apparent contradiction in their reports, the mother speaking of an improvement in her son's behavior although she had not followed instructions, and the teacher reporting a deterioration although she had done what she was asked to do. The psychologist couldn't decide whether the result was a failure on his part, or a solution of the problem. In any case, both women seemed much less worried about the boy than they had been before the psychologist's intervention.

Interventions of this type are, in any case, risks that should be taken only after a careful analysis of the context by a skilled psychologist certain of being in control of his relationships with others.

REFLECTIONS

Before the end of the school year, the director called a meeting of teachers. The agenda included—by agreement with the psychologist—an analysis of the team's work in the school. The psychologist, after giving a general account of the work done by the team, asked those present to voice their opinions on the team's contribution and point out any mistakes; their comments would prove helpful in planning the team's future activities. Despite this request, the only responses were expressions of appreciation for the work done and wishes that the team's activity could be extended to the rest of the school district. Only the director expressed some reservations. While he was full of praise for the psychologist, he criticized the psychomotor therapist. His objections were rooted in the symmetrical escalation at the beginning of the school year, which had obviously not yet been overcome. He repeated the same criticisms on other occasions.

From the various remarks, and from an analysis of the team's work in the school district, the team drew the following conclusions:

- The general opinions of those connected with the school about the team and its members depend on the relationship they manage to establish with the various groups in and around the school.

- The team's presence in a school can help to break rigid and repetitive relational patterns and encourage new relational models.

- The initial phase of the team's work in a school is of particular importance. Errors committed then are difficult to correct.

- In general, prior knowledge of conditions in the target school enable the team to prepare an adequate strategy and hence to avoid errors during the delicate initial phase.

- The most reliable and significant sign of the team's effectiveness in a school is its absorption in the relational system. A team that remains on the fringe cannot make a useful contribution. Neither can a team that gets drawn into factional disputes.

- A team member who is unable to control his relationship with people or groups within the school is bound to fail, since too much effort will go into defining and redefining the relationship.

- A team is absorbed into the school system most easily if it shows respect for the hierarchic structure, and if it includes every member of the system.

- In general, the process of absorption demands not only that a team be available and capable but also that the system in which it is to work be reasonably open. In some cases a team may be turned back at the very gates of a system. The only solution then is to try to identify the obstacles and surmount them. However, it can also happen that the system admits a team, only to relegate it to a small island, completely cut off from the mainland. That sort of polite relegation is reserved for illustrious guests whom the system wants to keep at bay. (In our case, this fate was reserved for the team by the teachers in the second school.)

■ Finally, a team is itself a system. Its operational capacity depends directly on its internal relationships. A team riddled with conflicts cannot work efficiently. But even a team that sets out well must constantly beware of being divided by maneuvers from outside.

THEORETICAL REFLECTIONS AND PRACTICAL SUGGESTIONS

THE ORGANIZATION PLAYS A GAME OF ITS OWN | 5

MARA SELVINI PALAZZOLI

A few decades ago family studies revealed to what extent the family group presents the research worker and the therapist with problems quite distinct from those found in an *ad hoc* group convened temporarily for experiment or therapy.

Writing about investigations based on *ad hoc* groups in his essay "Systemic Research on Family Dynamics," J. Framo admits that "without intending to detract in any way from the great value and contribution of *ad hoc* group research, and keeping in mind that everyone must bring at least part of his unique personality *sui generis* to any situation," he had concluded that such studies were of no help to the family therapist.[1] When we move from experiment to therapy, the distinction between *ad hoc* group therapy and family therapy becomes even more obvious. A group analyst who brings together strangers for treatment can watch as, step by step, group phenomena emerge from the incipient relational organization, or game.

By contrast, as the pioneers of family treatment came to realize, *families present the specialist with an existing, complex*

113

relational organization that is very hard to decipher. During their common history, the members of a family have gradually elaborated, by trial and error, their own mode of coexistence and of adaptation to the pressures of the environment. Congruent interdependence in inner functioning and in interactions with the environment has enabled the family to construct its own game, its own *mode of being itself.* It is the particular expression of such a mode that confronts the therapist.

The position of the psychologist encountering an organization is no different. An organization is a structured system characterized by the congruent functioning of its parts. These can be identified in the game it plays, reflecting the complex dynamics of coexistence both inside the system and outside. Therefore the specialist looks upon an organization as a relational model at work—more difficult to decipher than a family since it has more components and variables. To illustrate that point, I shall now examine the case we discussed at the outset, that of a company.

Its game had started long before the psychologist arrived, and its complexity rendered it inscrutable at first. Some aspects were displayed quite publicly: the modern enterprise, pioneering in the field of technical development and modernization, whose two owners had appointed an expensive, high-level management team to streamline the company. However, another game was being played behind the scenes—an antagonistic game that belied the myth of progressive management. The appointment of the psychologist came at a phase of the overall game when a move had to be made that satisfied the demands of appearances while not violating the obscurity behind the scenes.

The other organizations discussed in this book seem also to have established their own games well before the specialists were brought in.[2]

Our study points up another factor whose importance must never be underestimated, given its possible negative consequences: the previous experiences of that organization with other psychologists. Recall the pediatrics department and the school system. The two psychologists at the hospital had been preceded by a colleague who left a very poor impression (and consequently a stereotyped view of the entire profession). This caused the peculiar reception of the two psychologists, and they needed a great deal of tact to change it. The team assigned to the school district had also been preceded by "occasional" colleagues, who appeared irregularly and then simply vanished. In that case the team, duly alerted, took correct countermeasures: from the outset, it had a precise schedule and an office for its exclusive use.

A psychologist assigned to an organization must always begin work by collecting the information needed to frame verifiable hypotheses on relationships and to work out a viable approach. He must also find out what experiences the organization may have had with other psychologists, so he can prevent his work from being tainted with the legacy of his predecessors.

SIMILAR GAMES IN DIFFERENT ORGANIZATIONS

Our group set out with the idea that every situation had special features; but after about two years of research it became clear that these features were connected by a kind of thread. In fact, a detailed analysis of the different situations in which the psychologists found themselves began to reveal three recurring patterns:

A. *The psychologist is asked to join the organization by a loser who couples his invitation with an implicit offer of a coalition against someone.*

The loser can be a person, a group, or a subgroup. Moreover, he need not be an actual loser; it is enough that he should perceive himself as one, or fear that he is becoming one.

B. *In certain sociopolitical circumstances, the organization may create expensive structures simply to promote an appearance of change.*

After some time, these structures will manifest the following features:

- A proliferation of unimplemented projects.

- Rifts and factional struggles over various pet projects.

- The appearance of "symptoms" in one or more people.

C. *Manifest disagreements at the top of an organization may help that level to maintain control.*

Such disagreements are quickly resolved whenever anything happens to endanger control from the top.

Ecological review of case histories

What I propose to do now is to review the development of our case histories with the help of these three observations. However, I shall also consider the relevant social context, because an organization develops inseparably from its environment. E. Morin (1977) has insisted on this point:

> The environment is not merely co-present, it is also a co-organizer. The ecological aperture is not just a window on the environment; the organization, being an open system, does not fit into the environment as a mere part into a whole. The organization and the environment, while distinct from each other, are in each other, each in its own way, and their inseparable interactions and mutual relations are complementary, concurrent, and antagonistic. The environment both nourishes and threatens, brings into being and destroys. The organization, for its part, transforms, pollutes, and enriches.

This is obvious from the theoretical point of view, but hard to put into practice, always for the same reason: complex phenomena are hard to understand. Let us at once add another variable, time, whose importance must never be underestimated. Everything we observe in an organization at a given moment can be considered the climax of a chain of actions and reactions in which we (arbitrarily) identify the starting point of a particular environmental event that we consider pragmatically important. For example, in the case of the school system, that point was the admission of handicapped children into regular classes.

The psychologist's attempt to fashion a broader approach has interesting consequences. The first is a sometimes radical change in viewpoint—no longer arbitrarily focusing on the organization as a singular entity. The second is the abandonment of the value judgments that can fatally flaw narrow viewpoints, reducing reality to mere slices of reality.[3]

But let us proceed with our cases: the company, the teacher-training center, the pediatrics department, and the school district.

Pattern A: The psychologist is hired at the behest of the loser with the implicit offer of a coalition against somebody.

Since the prevailing mode of internal and external interaction predates the psychologist's arrival, it follows that his appointment must be a specific move in a wider game. Such moves are often made by the losing or hard-pressed party, who is seeking an ally to help him reverse his position. Hence it is important for the psychologist to discover who first suggested his appointment. But this information is difficult to obtain and often disguised or deliberately confused. In another case studied by our group, the psychologist at an institute for motor-impaired children was told that she had been called in at the request of the paramedical staff, who were having difficulties with the children and their parents. But during her first meeting with the director, he invited her to form a coalition against his assistant, "a dead weight, who blocks all my initiatives." From his attitude, our group inferred that bringing in a psychologist was in fact his idea, and that this particular game had more players than appeared at first sight.

The company

The origins of the situation that brought the psychologist into the company discussed in the first chapter could be traced back to the events of the preceding few years, especially the rapid expansion —the acquisition of new factories and a vastly increased staff. By all accounts, the growth caused many tensions that upset the existing structures. Moreover, during these years (it was after 1968), the burgeoning Left had insisted on expanded workers' rights, not just higher wages. An overhaul of management structure was therefore urgently needed, which meant loosening up the old form of management, in which the owners controlled all the information on the internal affairs of the company and made all the decisions. Loosening up meant delegating decisions to the managerial levels, circulating information to all levels, and encouraging greater staff participation.

In the past, the partners had reacted to such pressures for innovation by hiring experts in planning and management control. Presumably such projects would threaten the partners' exclusive control over the company. That threat was averted by means of a ploy: the president continued hiring more people to reform the company, while the vice-president boycotted the reforms with equal regularity. We do not know (and from the systemic point of view, it does not really matter) whether the ploy was deliberate or arose spontaneously from the reactions of these two men to the course of events. What interests us here is the effect of the interaction at work, since it put the new staff into a double bind: "Your high salary shows that the company considers your projects important—but they will never be implemented." The psychologist was appointed when internal unease had assumed embarrassing proportions (such as the resignation of the chemist) and had, moreover, begun to destroy the image the company tried to present. The game played at the top, which blocked every "dangerous" innovation, had begun to unleash a series of increasingly uncontrollable events, as happens in open systems in which a small input can trigger major chain reactions. An unacceptable increase in staff turnover, along with protests and incidents inside and outside the company, drew too much attention. As a result, the idea of appointing an industrial psychologist was conceived.

Despite their contradictory declarations and behavior, the two partners were clearly in substantial agreement about the appointment. In fact, it was the vice-president who, despite his later coolness, had proposed an acquaintance for the post, and who made the following revealing remark: "Nowadays, no company can call itself a model enterprise unless it bends over backwards to pamper the staff." What are we to make, then, of the president's inviting the psychologist to join him in a coalition? Throughout the period when our group was involved with this case, we were struck by the apparent disagreement of the two partners. At this level the offer of coalition seemed to make sense. The president was trying, with the psychologist's help, to get control of the production department run by the vice-president. Moreover, by issuing a cryptic suggestion to the psychologist to "pay particular attention to those individuals who undermine company morale," the president was clearly alluding to his partner, who, by ignoring the experts he had appointed (for example, the chemist hired to reform the purchasing department), drove them to frustration and depression. In short, the president seemed to be a loser keen to enter into a coalition against the victor—his partner. On the other hand, the vice-president had proposed one of his own acquaintances for the post, and asked him to concern himself exclusively with the administrative sector, so badly run by his partner.

Now, knowing the outcome (the acquisition of the only rival

company in the field), we can see that *the coalition was, in fact, offered by both partners* against the same enemy—the innovators who called for change and caused incidents likely to tarnish the image the company presented in order to attract capital. It is quite possible that from the economic point of view, expanding the company and acquiring a powerful competitor were not so much ambitious objectives as a matter of survival—not an unusual imperative.

Seen in this light, "those individuals who undermine company morale" (the president's words) and the "mediocre people who are too ambitious, and therefore quite useless to the company" (the vice-president's) were themselves: the two partners who were equally afraid of losing everything because of the innovators' demands.

Appointing an industrial psychologist fulfilled complex objectives. First, it advertised to the outside world: "Look how much this company cares about the psychological well-being of its staff." It said the same thing inside the company to staff members unaffected by the situation. As for those that suffered from it and complained, the psychologist could put their minds at ease by treating their symptoms (rather than by curing the roots of the disease). But above all—and from my point of view this was his essential function—*the psychologist's presence served to label all those who appealed to for help as "clinical cases."* This interpretation alone provides a convincing explanation of why the company appointed a staff psychologist instead of using an outside consultant. In the president's view, the company itself had no real problems to submit to a consultant: it merely needed a "doctor" to tend depressed or unbalanced employees. This was precisely how the president put it to the psychologist at their first meeting.

The In-Service Training Center (INSET)

In this case, the psychologist's appointment was a purely political move. This could be deduced from the mere fact that the center was founded at the instigation of the then-ruling party. The more immediate impetus was the conflict between the new director and his predecessor. The method of selecting the psychologist and his interview with the new director, related in Chapter 2, form a model illustration of Pattern A.

The pediatrics department

The decision of the director of the university research center to send two psychologists to this department did not as such involve any offer of a coalition against anyone. The two were ostensibly engaged as research workers. But they joined the department when the political struggles that had been raging in the hospital for several years had caused a radical shift in the old balance of power. The most obvious result had been a belittling of the chiefs of the various hospital departments. That was why the two successive heads of the pediatrics department made it clear to the psychologists that all other members of the department would be excluded from the decision-making process. In essence, therefore, the psychologists were invited to join a coalition against those who challenged the authority of the chiefs.

The school system

In this case, the appointment of the team could be traced back to the legislative decision to admit handicapped children to regular classes. That decision had caused many problems in previous years and resulted in the emergence of factions among the families and the teachers. The services of a psychologist had been demanded for some time by all sectors of the school system, the pro and con factions each hoping that he would side with them. In short, the pros hoped he would speed the admission of handicapped children, the cons that he would declare against this "impossible" measure. The local politicians, with elections approaching, felt that the time had come to prove their benevolence by supporting the admission of handicapped children. But the actual offer of coalition was made to the psychologist by the chairman of the school board, himself the father of a gravely handicapped child. The coalition was to be directed against the teachers and families who were against the proposal.

Pattern B: The organization may create expensive structures simply to promote an appearance of change.

In these structures, the following recurrent phenomena appear after an interval:

- A proliferation of unimplemented projects.

- Rifts and factional struggles over various pet projects.

- The appearance of "symptoms" in one or more people.

Pattern B reflects the existence of a permanent link in the chain of interactions between organizations and their environment.

An organization will show a desire for change as soon as the prevalent social ideology favors change. However, the very act of setting up a planning department shows both a wish for change and an assumption that changes *are bound to take time.* The result may be effectively a moratorium, a signal of the intention to delay any changes as long as possible, or the wish to make changes of an as yet unspecified kind. But this uncertainty does not affect the definition of the relationships involved, which is firmly anchored in the very existence of a planning department (*"My* department is the one that plans all the changes around here!").

The recurrent phenomena of Pattern B need time to manifest themselves. A planning department invariably starts work with enthusiasm, even euphoria, which takes a long time to die down. When the phenomena appear—abandoned projects, factional struggles, symptoms—it is a sign that this game has reached a critical point where it has lost its stabilizing function.

The company

The political need to appoint specialists to plan changes, and the mechanisms used to impede them, have been described above. The psychologist was appointed when the partners' game had reached a crisis and was about to lose its stabilizing function. The phenomena observed within the company fully corroborate our Pattern B.

The In-Service Training Center (INSET)

The origins of this body can be traced back to the reactions of Party A to the student revolution of May 1968. Rank-and-file members clamored for educational reform. The desire for change was demonstrated by the creation of an organization for educational reform, which continued on a fairly even keel until the election of Party B. Then Party B, to the left of Party A and therefore more inclined to radical innovation, found itself in an embarrassing situation when it came to implementing reforms. On the one hand, it felt the expectations of the rank and file, who believed that their time had come at last; on the other hand, it lacked the experience of Party A, and so preferred to stall. Therefore, the party appointed a head of the Department of Education who would be doomed to failure because, not being a party member, he would not have union support. In fact, he was meant to serve as a scapegoat should the situation become intolerable. For eighteen months the center then degenerated into a "project factory." Note that developments in the INSET Center were identical with those we have described in the company, though the two institutions were quite different.

The phenomena of Pattern B did not occur, however, in the pediatrics department or the school system.

Pattern C. Obvious disagreements at the top aid the maintenance of control, but they can be quickly resolved if they come to pose a threat to control.

The paralyzing effect of rifts at the top is evident. By "control from the top" we mean control of the definition of the relationship with subordinates and control of decision-making. These two functions are simultaneous and inseparable. Rifts at the top go hand in hand with corresponding disagreements among subordinates, and such divisions can engender factional struggles that may end up by interfering with the control levers.

Rifts at the top are healed very rapidly in three circumstances:

- When the trouble spreads to large groups at the base.

- When the trouble can no longer be contained in the organization nor concealed from the outside world.

- When the game at the top is no longer needed because its objectives have been attained.

The company

The disagreement over the appointment of the psychologist lasted four years, until shortly before his dismissal, and was patched up very quickly by a series of decisions made at the top.

This occurred when there was a kind of mutiny by a large number of employees. Moreover, the psychologist's report disclosed that the partners' game was no longer secret. The solution was the drastic separation of the territories and jurisdiction of the two partners.

But this move did not come until after the fixed objective had been attained: the acquisition of a company which enjoyed a near-monopoly in its field. That acquisition rendered the parent company considerably less vulnerable to attacks from the outside. Once the two partners had gone their separate ways, a conservative climate was felt inside the parent company, now run exclusively by the president, who had previously chased after innovation.

The new conservative climate in the company corresponded to a revival of conservatism on the sociopolitical scene, where the winds of change had been abating for some time.

The In-Service Training Center (INSET)

The disagreement at the top reflected the chronic political conflict between Parties A and B, which were, however, in substantial agreement about the need for gradual change. The source of the trouble was the disagreement between Party B, which had won the last round of elections, and their head of education, Dr. Aubier, who had transformed the center into a "project factory." While the troubles were confined to the staff, nothing changed, but as soon as it seemed that a large number of nursery-school teachers might push for changes, the disagreements were quickly resolved. Party B had no difficulty in getting rid of the inefficient official, replacing him with an extremely competent person. Parties A and B then reached agreement about the reorganization of the center, sharing all duties fairly. Here, too, the internal conflicts were resolved by a territorial separation: Professors Fontaine and Bariaud were each placed in change of separate centers, and there was satisfaction all around. It was now possible to proceed to the implementation of a feasible project.

The phenomena covered by Pattern C were not observed in the pediatrics department or the school system.

My ecological review of the cases presented in this book poses a question. The reader will have noticed that Pattern A applied to all four organizations, while Patterns B and C applied only to two. The probable reason is that the pediatrics department and the school system were parts of larger institutions. Programs for innovation were not devised by them but handed down from on high. What little control they themselves wielded was confined to routine matters. Hence the need to effect desirable changes and to control them would be felt less there than at a higher level.

THE PSYCHOLOGIST MUST CONSIDER HIS OWN ROLE | 6

LUIGI ANOLLI

As they evolve, organizations develop structural and functional characteristics determined by the existence of objectives (explicit and implicit), by the character of their structure (official or tacit), and by the characteristics of their particular "product." Every organization is further defined by the quality and quantity of its resources, by the flow of information (rational and metarational, such as beliefs, traditions, myths, ideologies), by the network of rules and metarules, and also by the distribution of decision-making powers.

However, organizations, as we have seen, are also characterized by the existence of specific relational games which evolve in step with external and internal changes. Often, such games contain conflictual factors, tensions, splits, and factional struggles accompanied by overt alliances and secret coalitions between groups or individuals.

The position of a psychologist, whether invited to join an organization or assigned to it, is no less complex. Even before he enters into preliminary discussions and examines the prospects of working in an organization, *he must take stock of his opinions and his personal and professional history*—in short, of his own attitudes. This chapter will consider the psychologist as a subsystem interacting within a given context.[1]

THE PSYCHOLOGIST AND THE ORGANIZATION AS A SUPERSYSTEM

It is a commonplace to state that the first contact—even by telephone—between the psychologist and the representatives of the organization he will work in sets up a circular system of communication between them: consciously or not, the two exert complex influences on one another, which determine the outcome of their negotiations and the quality of their later relationship.

To draw attention to this elementary, often neglected, fact means stressing that the psychologist is not a passive figure, but, from the outset, an active participant in all events, perhaps even in spite of himself. It would be a mistake to think that the representatives of the organization alone decide the outcome of the negotiations and the nature of the psychologist's contribution.

It is wrong to think that the organization is *here* and the psychologist is *there*. On the contrary, from their very first contacts, organization and psychologist constitute a single supersystem comprising two subsidiary systems, albeit with few relational links. That situation is reflected in the collaboration of the psychologist with public organizations (municipalities, sociomedical services, etc.), where the supersystem continues to function even after the politician who launched the research disappears from the scene.

The relational field defined by the supersystem is a continuous flux of verbal and nonverbal messages that influence the two interacting systems. Hence the psychologist must repeatedly ask himself *which of his responses* (verbal or nonverbal) *could have influenced the development of the situation in one direction rather than another.*

He asks the question not for moral reasons, but to examine the development of the interactions and to learn from it. In order to be precise in the examination, the psychologist must first delineate the various interactional sequences, starting *systematically with himself.* This will be more difficult for him the more disappointing the results are, since it runs counter to the general tendency to place blame on others.

But above all, this approach will teach the psychologist that *the only behavior that he can change directly is his own.* In a professional context, it is up to the psychologist, who has the theoretical and technical knowledge needed to assess the situation rapidly, to change it with the help of the only thing he has the power to change: his own behavior (for example, by responding to boastful behavior with a show of modesty, to prevent symmetrical escalation).

THE PSYCHOLOGIST IS HIS OWN INSTRUMENT

The central fact of the psychologist's professionalism is that, in his consulting capacity, *he is his own professional instrument.* Wundt anticipated this view when he defined psychology as the "science of direct experience"—experience not mediated by other instruments.

This applies particularly to the psychologist's professional approach. In the relatively simple situation of the clinical session with a client, even the inexperienced psychologist can observe changes in verbal and nonverbal reactions to his successive modes of communication. In fact, different styles of communication—amicable or pompous, emphatic or detached, neutral or ironic—produce markedly different responses during discussions; for example, a client will refer to personal problems much more frequently if the psychologist adopts a receptive attitude (Heller, 1968).

This doesn't mean that the psychologist must don a variety of masks; that would weaken his credibility, integrity, and effectiveness. It simply means that, while accepting his own emotional reactions, he has learned to filter them out and arrive at the appropriate response in a given context. Moreover, the psychologist, as a transmitter of verbal and nonverbal communications, should (cautiously) vary his style and observe the reactions of his interlocutors. Analyzing any differences would reveal important information and enable him to assess the situation better. This method, though far from simple, is a precondition for gathering valuable professional experience.

However, the psychologist is also a receiver, in which capacity he must respond spontaneously to messages from his interlocutors. But were he not to respond—a theoretical and practical impossibility—it would be a grave insult and might easily set off a symmetrical escalation. In a sense, the psychologist in an organization is on a par with his interlocutors and hence cannot help communicating on their level. But as his own professional instrument, he cannot help observing his interactions. In that sense, the concept of "objective" observation is obsolete. We subscribe to Morin's epistemological concept of observation (1977): Since, in the relationship between observing and observed system, the observer is as much part of the observed system as the observed system is part of the intellect and the culture of the observing system, Morin finds that *the observer observes himself while he observes the system.* The psychologist can observe the organization if he receives and decodes the information coming from it, and examines its reactions to changes in his own communications.

This first level of observation must be combined with a second level, or metalevel. Since all knowledge proceeds simultaneously towards both object and subject, the emergence of vicious circles can be avoided only by constructing a metasystem in which the observer observes himself while he makes his own observations. In other words, he should observe the incipient relationship between himself and his observations.

If he does, he should be able to keep a constant critical eye on the flow of interactions and communications of which he is a part. With the information thus obtained, he should be able to devise an appropriate strategy of communication, choosing forms of behavior that tend to foster a satisfactory and creative interpersonal relationship (thus avoiding circular patterns), and thus increase the possibilities of learning.

In sum, to assert that the psychologist is his own professional instrument is not to say that he must be nothing but his own authentic Rogerian self flowing with empathy and filled with trust and unconditional positive feelings towards others. Nor does it mean that the psychologist is merely a technician with a "recipe book" of interventions and strategies. On the contrary, it means that the psychologist, participating actively and skillfully in relationships on the basis of information he has collected in context, should be able to find—to invent—appropriate forms of behavior, response, or suggestion. This involves constantly choosing and constructing new solutions, and always reconsidering the developing interpersonal relationship.

SELF-KNOWLEDGE AS RELATIONAL KNOWLEDGE

It follows that the psychologist's professionalism depends on a sound understanding of the methods of interaction he employs. This understanding begins with *constant observation and deliberate analysis of the strategies of communication* he uses. Introspective "self-analysis" based on examining one's own feelings, impulses, and values is not the proper way to acquire such self-knowledge. Other authors have stressed that such self-analyses, no matter how long and sophisticated, are misleading because they tend to confirm a self-image built up during childhood and adolescence. They almost inevitably introduce distortions, since one is bound unconsciously to try to reconcile the self-image with any discordant elements. The psychologist's best means of acquiring this kind of relational self-knowledge is to observe the methods of communication he employs most frequently in his private and professional relationships.

This brings us to the fundamental concept of *relationship,* which is of crucial importance even in such branches of psychology as the study of perception. Our perception of objects is not absolute, all forms of perception (of color, size, movement, sound, etc.) are relative and based implicitly on systematic comparisons of two or more sensory data. The most elementary form of perception is that of a relationship—between figure and ground: there is no figure without a background, and vice versa.

In clinical psychology, psychoanalysis was the first to base the treatment of persons said to be neurotic on the elaboration of an important relationship—between therapist and patient—stressing the importance of transference and countertransference, which are largely repetitions of learned relational patterns. Later clinical approaches—Gestalt therapy, hypnotherapy based on M. Erickson's method, family therapy, etc.—have also stressed the decisive importance of relationships in the interaction between therapist and patient (Haley, 1963).

In the realm of theoretical research, the classic study by Wynne and Singer (1963) of possible common styles of communication (and hence of relating) in families of schizophrenic patients has shown that the contents of the communications are insignificant, while the style is crucial. During the most difficult and sophisticated phase of this research, Singer found statistically significant correlation of the results of Rorschach and TAT tests of young schizophrenics with those of their parents, based not only on the content of the responses (which proved "misleading") but also on the styles (formal models) of communication. Wynne and Singer hypothesized that such styles of communication were learned by schizophrenics in the family context.

Clearly the psychologist must pay careful attention to the relational styles he uses with others. In what way, for instance, does he react to aggressive communications? Or to a seductive tone of voice? What attitude does he usually adopt in the face of dismissive responses? How does he react to a challenging tone? Can he respect reticence? Is he inclined to persist doggedly, or does he prefer to close up, adopting a frustrated, unhappy expression? What effect does contempt produce on him, or fastidiously obsequious approaches? How does he react to long silences or to monotonous and boring conversations? How does he behave when his interlocutor seems aloof, defensive, or evasive? What method of communication will he adopt in the face of tears, despair, or urgent appeals?

Ideally, he ought to draw up a kind of map of relational models he uses most often in given situations.

THE LEARNING CONTEXT

By getting to know ourselves better through the observation of our own methods of communication and of our reactions to the communications of others, we also come to grips with our own "learning context."

Bateson was the first to elaborate this concept in his theoretical analysis of the phenomenon of learning, based on the theory of logical types.[2] Considering learning in the broader sense of a "change of some kind," he distinguishes successive levels of learning, ranging from Zero Learning to Learning III.

For Bateson, learning is inseparably linked with context (a fundamental concept in his epistemological system), in the sense that *no learning is conceivable outside a context of repeated events* (an experimental laboratory, a classroom, a family, etc.). He maintains, rightly, that without the hypothesis of repeated events, all learning must have a purely genetic basis. Bateson employs *context* as a generic term covering all the events from which the organism concludes that it has several alternatives from which to select those that will guide its behavior.

For our work, Bateson's concept of Learning II, or deutero-learning, is most important. In a lecture given in 1942 in which he began to develop this concept, Bateson defined it thus: "If . . . we inflict a series of similar learning experiments on the same subject, we shall find that in each successive experiment the subject has a somewhat steeper proto-learning gradient, that he learns somewhat more rapidly. This progressive change in rate of proto-learning we will call 'deutero-learning.' "[3] In other words, the subject manages bit by bit and with decreasing effort to reach a goal or to pass a test. In 1964 Bateson defined successive levels of learning in accordance with the theory of logical types:

- Zero Learning is the immediate base of all those acts which are not subject to correction by trial and error.

- Learning I is the revision of choice within an unchanged set of alternatives.

- Learning II is the revision of the set of alternatives from which the choice is to be made.

- Learning III is the corrective revision of the system of the sets of alternatives from which the choice is made. It is a change in the process of Learning II, a kind of reconstruction of the learning context (as in psychotherapy, in religious conversion, in any self-transformation).

Let us consider Learning II, then look briefly at Learning III. It is important to recall that the concept of "learning context" refers not to individual qualities and characteristics, but to exchanges between the individual and his environment. Hence, to assert that "A depends on B" means that their relationship is characterized by the sequence a_1, b_1, a_2, where a_1 is seen as a signal of weakness, b_1 as a helping act, and a_2 as an acknowledgment of b_1.

Beyond being an analytical instrument for the study of human interactions, the learning context must be seen as a fundamental mode of *punctuating sequences of events,* and of *attaching special significance to them,* without a very highly structured stimulus-response mechanism.

Illustrations can readily be found in Part One of this book. Thus the psychologist assigned to the school district, before preparing his overall strategy, had to assess his own confidence vis-à-vis a director known to be authoritarian. He knew that, unlike the psychomotor therapist, he could tolerate authoritarian behavior. But if the director had been indecisive, low-key, or even querulous, our psychologist would have had to cope with a situation that *for him* would be much more difficult.

Such situations show how important it is for the psychologist to be conscious of his own learning contexts, which help define his "character." Bateson asserts that what we call "character" is the result of Learning II, which underlies many of our premises, habits, and other set attitudes.

However, in our view, the psychologist need not be aware of the finer details; all he needs to do is to grasp the essential features of his own learning contexts. This will enable him to identify the weak points and the strong points of his relational models and to bear them in mind in his professional life.

THE PSYCHOLOGIST'S PAST AND PRESENT

We might now look more closely at *the relationship between the past and the present in the history of an individual.*

According to general systems theory, every living system is the best "explanation" of itself at any given moment. This means that, to understand a living system, it is unimportant, indeed wrong, to search for causes that shaped it. Similarly, it would be wrong to try to discover its purposes or goals. The "finality" of a system is a quality that reflects the type of organization built up over time.

This theoretical approach involves the principle of "equifinality," which states that in living systems, precisely because they are more or less open and interact incessantly with a changing environment, similar causes can lead to different results, and different causes can lead to similar results. It follows that the situation of a system at a specific time cannot be meaningfully interpreted by reference to prior events or to "past causes."

Let us now look more closely at these two related concepts: learning context and personal history.

A personal history, inasmuch as it is a "reality," cannot of course be known on the psychological plane; it is a record of what was and is now gone, not of what is happening on the actual stage of life. But on the individual and social plane there is, however, a close connection between past and present, although they belong to different levels.

The present is the class of events covering but one aspect of the indefinite potential of a living system at a given moment in a given environment. These events are therefore characterized by maximum unpredictability.

The past, by contrast, is a class of events that have happened, that is, of completed situations. This is thus a state of maximum stability.

But although the past and the present belong to different logical levels, there is a link between them: *in living systems the present contains the past.* Ashby has shown that living systems use random processes to arrive at solutions that, adopted in past situations, have optimized their chances of success. Living systems are their own best explanations, precisely because they contain their past in themselves. This is as true of a unicellular amoeba as it is of a giant sequoia.

In general, we use the term "memory" to refer to this state of affairs from the outside; inside the system such interpretations are superfluous.

However, the present not only contains its "past history" but, being of a higher logical level, it also explains it. We can therefore say that *the present metacommunicates about the past* (Selvini Palazzoli, 1979). In fact, the present, understood as the historical expression of the individual at a given moment, represents a state of maximum information. That is why it provides the individual with the best criteria for "reading" and "understanding" his past. It is the more complex that explains the simpler, and not vice versa. We can therefore posit that present methods of communication are commentaries on past methods. This is where the idea of a learning context comes in, understood as a close, but not usually conscious, *link between the past and the present.*

Against this background, the perpetuation of *context markers* (signals of context recognition) acquires an important significance. In other words, what ensures the psychological identity and functioning of the individual is the *constancy of signals of context recognition.* They are indispensable criteria of observation, of decoding and analyzing the innumerable and varied relational contexts in which the individual can find himself.

As general examples of signals of context recognition, we may mention shaking hands (a sign of nonhostility), the nameplates on the doors of professionals (a sign of special competence), the raised platform in the classroom (a sign of the teacher's function). Thus, the arrangement of the offices of the president, vice-president, and staff in the company we discussed in Part One provided the psychologist with important clues. Similarly, the proliferation of meetings and projects at the In-Service Training Center during Dr. Aubier's tenure was an important pointer to its position at the time.

From such observations about the past and present of each individual, and hence also of the psychologist, it is possible to draw a number of conclusions regarding the latter's professional work in organizations.

- The psychologist must be able to *identify an adequate repertoire of context markers.* Too small a repertoire would hamper his ability to act.

- He must analyze the recognition signals of his own learning context in order to gain the flexibility he needs to adapt his own relational methods to new situations.

- When making contact with representatives of a new organization (or entering a new working environment), many psychologists tend to apply relational models that have been successful (or at least neutral) in other contexts. Clearly, this tendency can trigger a systematic series of errors, since strategies adapted to one context are not necessarily suitable for others.

  This explains why the initial phase demands *an adequate period of observation,* to allow the identification of the main recognition signals used in the new context. That involves framing hypotheses about rules in the new organization and being able to verify them. The fundamental importance of this initial phase of observation is borne out by all the experiences discussed in Part One.

■ On the strictly operational plan, the psychologist, aided by a the knowledge of his own learning context and by what information he has gathered, must gradually develop a capacity for correcting, choosing, and "keeping a record" of his own relational models in the light of new recognition signals. In other words, he must revise and reconstruct his own learning contexts. We shall be returning to this crucial point.

THE PSYCHOLOGIST'S MAIN LEARNING CONTEXTS

We can now comment on the psychologist's own learning contexts.

There is first of all the crucial contribution of *his own family*, from whom the psychologist—like every other individual—acquired his basic mode of relating to other people. Thus in his childhood he absorbed many rules of communication, and also such *metarules* as who has the right to set the rules, in what context, and so on. He thus acquired his main criteria (explicit and implicit) for dealing with various aspects of life. While he probably found some modes of communication conflictless and perfectly smooth, others caused him problems and conflicts—and he never even considered still others. Moreover, through interactions with his family, the psychologist acquired his self-image, self-esteem, and goals. In short, his family helped him to arrive at a more or less clear definition of himself.

It is obvious that the relational models learned in the bosom of the family are the deepest and most persistent of all, and hence have a most powerful effect on later professional actions.

The reader may remember the response of the psychologist, Mlle. Lanzi, when the director of the In-Service Training Center invited her to enter into an alliance (see Chapter 2). No doubt, having grown up in a simple but authoritarian family, and having learned the virtues of compliance there, she repeated that behavior when she met a person in authority who treated her in the same way in a similar context.

Learning contexts also account for the psychologist's professional "personality," which can be traced back to his training period—his entire school and university career, particularly his study of psychology. In these crucial years, the student is pressed into adopting a well-defined idea of what it means to be a psychologist. He is handed down explicit and implicit criteria of professional success (and failure).

This point is well illustrated by the behavior of the two young psychologists assigned to a pediatrics department (see Chapter 3). Coming from the university, they unconsciously carried a certain stamp of superiority. Their first attempt to work in the ward failed because they mistakenly assumed that the agreement between their professor and the chief of pediatrics would guarantee them the full support of the staff.

All in all, there is no doubt that the training of psychologists in Italy (and elsewhere) has grave shortcomings. Because of the large number of students, the inadequate facilities, the shortage of audio-visual aids, there is a real risk of providing students with nothing but booklearning, which, though necessary for the training of psychologists, is certainly not sufficient. The psychologist, even though fully trained, must amplify his learning with concrete experiences *in the field.*

There is no psychologist who does not recall with embarrassment the errors committed at the start of his professional career. Yet such errors are inevitable. The psychologist, like every other professional, must look to his own experience for guidance, and engage in the difficult process of discovering his own preferred relationship models.

This calls for a learning process based on trial and error, on systematic training and detailed verification of working hypotheses; it is, moreover, a repeated matching of one's professional ability to different situations. This approach helps the psychologist to see and learn from his mistakes, to articulate precise criteria of intervention leading to effective solutions, and to frame working hypotheses that can be discarded if they prove inconsistent or dangerous.

The professional attitude of the psychologist also generally reflects ideological overtones, to which we can only allude here. If these overtones exist at the theoretical level (Battacchi, 1972), they will exist all the more in the operational context. We need merely recall what happened in the 1970s, when it was fashionable to argue in psychological circles that institutions must be changed in order to change individuals. The ideological nature of that approach is apparent when we consider the preceding professional attitude, whose main objective was to change individuals in order to change institutions—or to adapt individuals to institutions.

All in all, when he first approaches an organization or starts work in a new setting, the psychologist never arrives as a neutral entity, but brings his own relational history and his whole personality with him.

This may, of course, be a great advantage inasmuch as it may introduce new ideas, perspectives, and hypotheses. But the psychologist can also repeat in the new context, rigidly and indiscriminately, ways of relating and communicating more appropriate to other contexts and times. Only by a gradual *process of assimilation and accommodation* can the psychologist become integrated into the new working environment. Assimilation involves elements known from other contexts; accommodation, by contrast, is the invention of operational schemes appropriate to the specific elements of the new context.

RESTRUCTURING THE PSYCHOLOGIST'S OWN LEARNING CONTEXT

To work successfully in a new organization with his particular personal and professional history, with his own criteria of analysis and intervention, and with the result of his own learning, the psychologist inevitably arrives at a point where he must adjust his own ways of relating to those of others. If he fails to do so he runs the risk of committing repetitive errors that will compromise or paralyze his activity.

Hence the experienced psychologist must be capable of making changes that fall into Bateson's category of Learning III. In other words, he must be able to learn to change the habits acquired by deutero-learning (Learning II). According to Bateson, Learning III, which few people can achieve, enormously amplifies the individual's relational potential. "To the degree that a man achieves Learning III, and learns to perceive and act in terms of the contexts of contexts, his 'self' will take on a sort of irrelevance. The concept of 'self' will no longer function as a nodal argument in the punctuation of experience." This could "lead to greater flexibility in the premises acquired by the process of Learning II—a *freedom* from their bondage."

No doubt the ability to restructure one's own learning contexts by revising the premises and relational modes implicit in them is a long, in some respects endless, process. But it is the royal road to helping others change their attitudes, when they need changing.

THE PSYCHOLOGIST AND THE PROBLEM OF HIERARCHIC LEVELS

7

VALERIA UGAZIO

One thing distinguishing large organizations, such as companies, hospitals, or schools, from families, and from *ad hoc* and informal groups, is their formalized hierarchic structure. That structure divides organizations into levels, defines the functions of each level and relationships between them, and sets rules governing the interaction of the organization with its environment. It thus limits the discretionary power of members in defining their relationships to one another. In other words, institutional interactions are bound by the hierarchic order.

However, the interrelations in other social groups, even informal ones, are also subject to certain constraints.

The history of a group, the rules it has gradually adopted, its specific character and that of its members, and the prevailing social norms are aspects that help determine the relationships of every social group. The very concept of organization presupposes the existence of links. According to Buckley (1967), the parts of an organized whole are linked together in a way that ensures that certain interrelations prevail rather than others. That means that

139

a group of elements, whether persons or things, becomes an organization the moment all the possible interrelations cease to have the same probability.

As Ashby (1962) has put it, "The organization of 'variables' involves the presence of links that limit its possibilities."

Moreover, in institutions, unlike informal groups, some of these links are immutable. The formalization of its hierarchy thus inevitably produces an ossification of an organization. It can therefore be said that if all its communication circuits and interrelations fit completely into the formalized hierarchic structure, the institution will be a static system incapable of adaptation, and hence of survival. That does not usually happen: the latent organizational chart never fully corresponds to the official organizational chart. Many interaction patterns found in institutions are not formalized —indeed, seem alien to the hierarchic structure. Similarly, the so-called "formal networks" of communication almost never faithfully follow the path mapped out by those at the top. However, too large a discrepancy between the manifest and the latent organizational charts will paralyze an organization. The existence of a hierarchic structure, even if it does not completely predetermine the relations within an organization, drastically curtails the freedom of its members to define their relationships.

The psychologist cannot escape these limitations. His encounter with an institution brings him face to face with an organized body that has developed its own "game," whose rules are partly predetermined by a fixed scheme. This scheme is none other than the hierarchy to which the psychologist is subjected in his interaction with the institution. It is his link with the hierarchy that most clearly distinguished the psychologist's work in an institution from that in his private office. His entry into an organization usually requires the acceptance of some form of hierarchic dependence, either on the institution in which he will work or on the institution that has appointed him. In both cases a great many rules defining his relationship with the client organization—from his schedule and pay to his objectives and methods—will be partly dictated by the institution.

When working out a strategy with the organization, the psychologist must therefore pay very careful attention both to the limitations imposed by the hierarchic structure and to the contractual possibilities left open to him. This rarely happens. On the one hand, a psychologist usually sees himself as an "independent professional" even in his work in an organization, and as a result underestimates his relationship with the hierarchy; or, more rarely, he exaggerates it to the point of believing that he has no freedom of action whatever. On the other hand, the vagueness of the organization's demands, and the frequently anomalous position it assigns to him, can easily lead him into mistaking the ambiguity of his role in the institutional context for autonomy from the hierarchy. Keep in mind that very few social workers, and hardly any psychologists, have had any preparation in dealing with the dynamics of systems. That shortcoming often persuades the psychologist to apply to institutions conceptual categories and models based on the psychoanalytical approach. The worst result may be that his field of competence is defined not by himself but by the organization, on the basis of its past experiences. In the best case, he may think himself able to plan and carry out work with all the freedom of a professional running his own office.

"It is very important and even fundamental that the school psychologist's every intervention should be in keeping with the hierarchic structure of the institution in which he works. The school authorities must be informed of, and agree to, every one of the psychologist's initiatives" (Selvini et al., 1976). The experience of our group not only confirms but extends these conclusions. Our analysis of the interaction between the psychologist and institutions with hierarchic structures even more complex than a school has convinced us that the psychologist must follow the hierarchic path, both during the contractual negotiations and when he seeks the organization's genuine agreement to his initiatives. He cannot afford to ignore the hierarchic structure in any of his contacts with the organization.

Our research revealed that many impasses between psychologists and institutions were due to the psychologist's failure to observe his position in the organization. Our research group, in several cases, proposed strategies of intervention which proved mistaken for the same reason.

From such "errors"—and from their effects—our group drew the fundamental conclusion that *the psychologist's operational strategy must be adapted in advance to his position in the hierarchic structure of an organization.* That position is quite variable, as the experiences discussed in Part One show. The reader may remember that in the case of the company, the psychologist was absorbed into the hierarchic structure. He had a full-time job and a place on the company's organizational chart. The psychologist working for the In-Service Training Center was also included in the organization. Unlike her colleague in the company, however, she worked in close collaboration with people on the same hierarchic level (psychologists and teachers). The situation of our psychologist in the suburban school district was quite different: he remained outside the chain of command. As he pointed out during his first contacts with the schools, he was in fact answerable to another institution, the municipality.

The various ways of joining an institution present a multitude of operational possibilities for the psychologist. We believe, therefore, that before forming a working program, he must first examine his place in the organization's structure. Based simply on that information, he will be able to gauge the suitability of his plans.

In particular, two choices with a crucial bearing on his efficiency depend closely on his place in the organization. The first concerns the *sphere of his intervention*—that is, the subsystems in which he will work. The second concerns the *program,* the type of intervention he can propose to those subsystems.

CHOOSING THE SPHERE OF INTERVENTION

When he first joins an organization, the psychologist, thanks to the ill-defined expectations placed on him, is theoretically often able to choose the subsystem to which he intends to direct his main activity. These subsystems range from the top of the organization to the intermediate strata, and in the case of services, to the users (in a school, the pupils and their parents; in a hospital, the patients). However, the psychologist's elbow room is not nearly as great as it first seems.

To begin with, the size and complexity of a large institution prevent him from observing the whole institution. Were he to attempt that, he would be swamped with unmanageable variables. It follows that he must confine his activity to accessible subsystems.

The existence of a formalized hierarchic structure imposes additional limits on his choice of the most suitable sphere of intervention. Our research group concluded that he cannot choose to act, explicitly or even implicitly, over the heads of the organization, nor in subsystems at his own hierarchic level.

In order to intervene effectively in a subsystem, the psychologist must first be able to occupy a "one-up" position for as long as necessary to assure that his own role remains viable. This one-up position is equally important when it comes to protecting the progress of his interventions.

Now it is precisely this kind of one-up, complementary relationship that the psychologist cannot possibly achieve with the top of the hierarchy or with colleagues. Adopting a one-up position would conflict with his place in the organization—dependent on the board or management, equal to his colleagues. So he will not be able, on joining an organization, to negotiate about methods of intervention involving these subsystems. Nor can he expect to change the original contract after he joins the organization. Were he able to intervene indirectly at the top or among his peers, he would soon confront insurmountable difficulties and eventually become a catalyst of communication breakdowns in the organization.

The company we discussed in Part One is an excellent case in point. The psychologist, upon his appointment, accepted the president's implicit request that he exclude the partners from his analysis of the company's difficulties. The original discussions concluded with the agreement that the psychologist would examine the conflicts in the company, not merely by focusing on employees' personal problems, as the president had originally asked, but also by examining the organizational context in which these problems appeared. But it was perfectly clear that the psychologist would have to be careful not to analyze the behavior of the partners or its effects on the employees. This was in keeping with his position of hierarchic dependence, a position emphasized by his full-time employment by the company.

However, at the request of our research group, the psychologist broke this agreement, the group having decided to adopt an interventionist stance. The group focused its attention on the repetitive game played by the president and vice-president.

The group and the psychologist then tried to put an end to this game by appropriate steps, including interventions at the top, which seemed imperative, since even if they did not lead to the required changes, they promised to provoke reactions that would have enabled the group to confirm or invalidate its hypothesis.

We decided on an indirect approach: the psychologist would use employees to convey messages to the partners that were likely to spur a change in company policy. An opportunity soon arrived: the request by the engineer (the second "patient") for help in tendering his resignation "with dignity." As the reader may remember, the psychologist carefully rehearsed with the engineer, impressing upon him the importance of giving a positive connotation, especially to the president's most absurd behavior.

The effects of this maneuver were disappointing on the whole. However, the psychologist pursued his objective. His support for the project by the "new manager"—to create task groups made up of the managers of various departments—reflected his wish to send the partners a further message likely to engender changes. The result was another failure. At this point the psychologist, whose exasperation was shared by our group, intervened directly by sending a report to the partners, in which he described their game, though he gave the game itself a positive connotation. He realized that this maneuver would seal his fate in the company: even if the two partners had not gone their separate ways (and even if there had been no changes in the company rendering the psychologist and many high-level managers superfluous), the psychologist would have had to go. By metacommunicating about the relational game at the top, he not only broke his original contract but, what mattered most, he also broke the rules governing its hierarchic structure. He had placed himself in a one-up position that was incompatible with his hierarchic dependency.

Moreover, his effectiveness had been undermined by his use of employees as go-betweens with the partners. In so doing, he had made the same fatal mistake as a family therapist who uses the very patterns of dysfunctional communication that he is trying to change.

The psychologist's behavior was, in fact, a reflection of the president's own. As we saw, the president had no business intervening in his partner's sector at the formal, hierarchic level. This was in keeping with the company's paradoxical inner structure. Similarly, the psychologist, metacommunicating about the conduct of the partners through his "patients," broke the rule of his own hierarchic dependency.

The discussion of this case led our group to abandon the unrealistic idea of treating the top echelon and the psychologist's peer group as targets of intervention for producing change. It was clear, moreover, that the psychologist's mistake was not so much wrong tactics as the very attempt to change the game at the top. Instead, he ought to have had a *single objective* in his dealings with the partners and his peers—to promote functional communications with them.

We also believe that even with other subsystems, the psychologist's *main task* is to act as a catalyst of functional communication: he must be careful to maintain the relationships in flexible equilibrium so as to avoid repetitive games. It is only when this balance is achieved that the psychologist will acquire the knowledge prerequisite to his effective intervention in subsystems. And it is in that sense that we first framed the hypothesis that the psychologist must be an expert whose professionalism "resides first of all in his ability to control his own behavioral communications in response to behavioral communications from the various subsystems of an organization."[1]

The group's more recent cases reflect this new strategy: in his dealings with his superiors and his peers, the psychologist must center his efforts on fostering functional communications between himself and the other subsystems.

This explains why the complex communicational maneuvers, both analogic and verbal, used by our educational psychologist in his dealings with the director of the school system were not aimed at changing the complementarity of the transactions between the director and the teaching staff, let alone at gaining the upper hand over the director. Their purpose was rather the creation, however laborious, of a relationship based on collaboration between the psychologist and the director as an indispensable step towards being accepted by the system.

Similarly, the sole aim of the psychologist at the INSET Center was to be accepted by her colleagues in the applied research sector. The psychologist's suggestion to these colleagues that they acknowledge their differences, a suggestion aimed at destroying the paralyzing myth of agreement at any price, showed that she herself was prepared to accept these differences.

All these interventions, although intended to facilitate the psychologist's work, had much wider repercussions. Thus, thanks to the good relationship he established with the school director, our educational psychologist was able to involve the teachers in various group experiments. These experiments introduced new learning methods that ran counter to the established decision-making process based on authoritarian leadership. Again, the vicious, competitive cycle of symmetrical reactions that had plagued the staff of the INSET Center was attenuated by the effective presence of the psychologist. Such results should not surprise anyone. They reflect the fact that a change in one sector of a system can cause much wider changes, thanks to the exchange of information.

AT WHAT LEVEL DOES THE PSYCHOLOGIST INTERVENE?

If a psychologist is to fit effectively into an organization, not only must he keep a constant watch on his own behavioral communications so as to keep a neutral position in the games of the various factions that invariably divide the institution, *but he must also submit a precise working proposal.* He must be able to clarify his function during the initial period if he hopes to play a useful part. A cryptic silence or evasive attitude on this subject has at least two deleterious effects:

- It increases unrealistic expectations.

- It engenders suspicions of all types, not least the fear that the psychologist is trying to usurp a superior position.

In fact, in the absence of a definite proposal, the work of the psychologist is out of control.

By failing to define his role unambiguously, especially in an institutional context, he adopts an equivocal position which can lead to his isolation. This was the case with the research psychologists in the pediatrics ward, whose original reticence about their objectives was alternately interpreted as snobbishness and as a cover for "spying."

After a period of preliminary observation, the psychologist must draw up a proposal, clearly indicating who will benefit and what concrete projects he hopes to execute. That proposal should serve as a basis for a general negotiation with the institution. While respecting the normal hierarchic channels, the negotiation must involve all parts of the organization. The proposal must precede every step the psychologist intends to take.

We have already listed those he can negotiate with. He must carefully explain the central aspects of his program and the type of intervention he proposes. In this case, too, he should pay great attention to and evaluate his specific position in the organization.

To simplify matters, we might say that there are two main types of intervention available to a psychologist working in an organization.[2]

The first, at the relationship level, focuses on the relational problems of the various subsystems of the organization, and between it and its clients. The psychologist must devise methods likely to resolve or diminish conflicts based on the definition of the relationship between the parties. These conflicts, although they rarely cause a complete collapse of the organization, may nevertheless block its decision-making process and drastically reduce productivity.

The second form of intervention by the psychologist, which we call a "technical consultation," is based completely on the level of the content. By content, in this case we mean the psychologist's particular area of expertise (such as education). The psychologist places this competence at the disposal of the organization, or of the subgroups that ask for it, and organizes suitable initiatives (lectures, courses, personnel selection, etc.).

For a long time, our research group believed that these two forms of intervention were at variance, that one was centered *exclusively* on relationships, the other *exclusively* on content. We realized later that this apparent conflict was formal rather than functional. Just as every communication on relationships has a content aspect, so every initiative, even if centered on content, has a relational aspect.

Nevertheless, the choice the psychologist makes between these two levels of communication has important consequences. Intervening explicitly in the relationships of a subsystem requires the psychologist to be first of all a consultant. If the psychologist is part of the organization he cannot work explicitly at the relationship level, since he cannot assume a "metaposition" towards the subsystems, which is imperative when intervening in relationships.

Furthermore, not even the position of consultant is ideal. Surely it is not the best position from which to avoid conflicts with top management.

It is difficult to maintain a position that is simultaneously high enough and neutral enough to intervene in relationships. The psychologist generally works with those in the lower hierarchic subsystems, individuals who cannot choose their psychologist themselves. And because he is dependent on the heads of the organization, he has limited room to accept or reject management's requests for his intervention.

Our work has convinced us that psychologists working in organizations should explicitly center their programs of intervention on content—i.e., on their technical expertise. Yet with a program of that type, the psychologist is not precluded from intervening at the level of relationships. Rather, he puts that aspect of his intervention on an implicit, nonverbal level, which is the most effective, and, by its very nature, the least subject to rejection.

DENIED COALITIONS | 8

PAOLA DI BLASIO

The subject of denied coalitions, which has been largely ignored in the study of organizations, is well known to family therapists. The first to look into the matter—as a relational method characteristic of pathological systems—was J. Haley. He considers it a fundamental element of perverse triangles, defined as follows:

- The people in the triangle are not peers; instead, one of them is of a different *generation*, a different order in the power hierarchy, such as parent and child, or manager and employee.

- The person of one generation forms a *coalition* with the person of the other generation against his peer. By "coalition" is meant a joint action *against* the third person (in contrast to an *alliance*, in which two people share a common interest, independent of a third person).

- Though there is certain behavior indicating a coalition, if it is queried, the coalition will be *denied*. [1]

149

An *alliance for* is an association of two or more persons in pursuit of a common interest. In overt conflicts, there may also be *alliances* of some *against* others. Alliances, unlike denied coalitions, are freely admitted, indeed openly declared, even when they involve different generations. Thus a father can openly ally himself with his son to help him overcome the effects of his mother's excessive anxiety.

DENIED COALITIONS AND THE PSYCHOLOGIST

The cases presented in Part One show that a psychologist can often detect signs of denied coalitions between various members of an organization he is joining. He not only will be unable to change such relationships but will be prevented from evaluating them correctly. What he *can* do is evaluate the developing relationship between himself and the game played by the organization. Thus he may receive offers of a coalition; if these are denied, the denials are signs of a critical situation. As we have stressed in our analysis of methods used to hire psychologists, the offer of a coalition implies the existence of a losing party, or one that feels endangered and seeks help in reversing the situation. Such offers, if the psychologist can decode and foil them, enable him to introduce alternative learning contexts (see Chapter 6). If not, the psychologist risks legitimizing certain ways of acting and may become enmeshed in them himself. We believe that a psychologist must be able to control his own behavioral responses in order to encourage interactions free of old patterns, and thus useful as spurs to learning, so any involvement in denied coalitions would assuredly damage his prospects.

CHARACTERISTICS OF OFFERS OF DENIED COALITIONS

What makes a discussion an offer of a denied coalition? What restrictions does the acceptance of denied coalition impose on the psychologist?

We can speak of an offer of denied coalition when:

- The proposal of *alliance for* is vague and general, lacking concrete objectives.

- The interactions is purely dyadic—there are only two parties.

- The messages, especially the nonverbal ones, hint at the existence of a secret that has to be kept.

These three phenomena must occur simultaneously.

By way of illustration, let us examine the offer of a denied coalition by Professor Fontaine of the INSET Center to Mlle. Lanzi, the psychologist (see Chapter 2). All three conditions appeared during their interview. In particular, Professor Fontaine masked his request for a coalition behind "screen" requests regarding the efficiency of the center, thus ostensibly proposing an *alliance for* His arguments rendered disagreement impossible: you are bound to approve of those who seek greater efficiency and to disapprove of those who shirk their obligations ("people who are paid for forty hours but put in only ten," as Professor Fontaine phrased it). Ostensibly he was asking the psychologist to work hard and to join him in an alliance to improve the service, albeit in vague and unspecified ways. He made the interview private, almost secret; the discussion could not have included third parties, and was meant to be purely dyadic. By continual implicit references to those who obstructed the service, he implied that the psychologist must surely share his aims and ideology, thus introducing the inclusion and exclusion mechanisms characteristic of dyadic relationships. To Professor Fontaine it was self-evident that their positions were identical and that he could count on the psychologist's full support. The presence of third parties would have altered the messages; they would then have been seen not as an invitation to join an exclusive relationship, but as an offer of alliance *against* those responsible for inefficiency.

Only in a dyadic conversation is it possible to allude to absent persons without spelling things out, while hinting that it all must be kept secret. Acquiescing to such insinuation means getting entangled in a secret coalition, which, as we have said, will severely limit one's freedom of action. In particular:

- The psychologist cannot define his own relationship with other members of the institution.

- Because of the nature of the messages exchanged in denied coalitions, the psychologist forfeits his ability to foster functional communications, since he has to guard his own behavioral responses.

- The psychologist is doomed to lose one of his most powerful operational tools, namely, the structuring of collaborative situations. *Denied coalitions make for confusing behavior.*

As an illustration of the first point, let us return to the case of the teacher training center. Clearly, had the psychologist joined a denied coalition with Professor Fontaine against Dr. Bariaud, she would have been able to define her own relationship with the latter and his allies only by respecting the rules of the denied coalition; indeed, Professor Fontaine would have been the one to define the psychologist's relationship with Dr. Bariaud. Now, to leave the definition of one's relationships to others means leaving a large vacuum that others will hasten to fill.

The drawback associated with the second point is analogous to a similar phenomenon often seen in perverse family triangles: the concurrence of messages that confirm the existence of the coalition at one level, while denying it at another. The members of the coalition *against* become involved in a double game of having to both confirm and reject one another even while confirming and rejecting those against whom the coalition was formed. Messages that seem to deny the coalition are meant to reassure those who are excluded from it, showing that nothing is being done against them. Precisely the same thing happens in perverse family triangles, when the son who has fallen into the trap of a coalition *against* seems unable to decipher the tissue of contradictory messages he receives, so that he begins to doubt his own perceptions. For example, when a mother covertly communicates to her son how much she suffers from some of her husband's actions, she may cause the son to turn against his father. But if he does, the mother, far from approving, may chide him for his lack of affection and respect.

Obviously, if the psychologist becomes involved in denied coalitions, he will be prevented from doing his main job. It is impossible to foster functional communications with others or between them if your own are ambiguous.

The impossibility of defining relationships and fostering communications prevents the psychologist from structuring stable contexts of collaboration, and thus from dealing with problems he is meant to solve.

This is because denied coalitions involve accepting the implicit rule that the context will remain unstable and precarious. Thus, a covert coalition with the director of a school against a group of teachers will mean the psychologist cannot guarantee the stability of the context, because he accepts *a priori* that his relationship with the teachers will differ according to whether the director is present. Moreover, caught in the game of simultaneously confirming and denying the coalition, he will send verbal messages defining the context in one way, while sending nonverbal messages contradicting them. Such situations produce a phenomenon similar to that which Bateson has described in connection with classic learning experiments. He points out that in Pavlov's work on experimental neuroses,

> The information "This is a context for discrimination" is communicated at the beginning of the sequence and *underlined* in the series of stages in which discrimination is made progressively more difficult. But when discrimination becomes impossible, the structure of the context is totally changed. The context markers (e.g., the smell of the laboratory and the experimental harness) now become misleading because the animal is in a situation which demands guesswork or gambling, *not* discrimination. The entire experimental sequence is, in fact, a procedure for putting the animal in the wrong at the level of Learning II. In my phrase, the animal is placed in a typical "double bind" which is expectably schizophrenogenic.[2]

Despite the obvious differences introduced by the laboratory situation, this scheme can also be applied to human interactions. For example, when the solution of a problem brings the psychologist in contact with teachers against whom he has joined a coalition, he can initially mark the context as collaborative, but as soon as anything impinges on his coalition with the director, he will find it very hard to preserve the collaboration. At one level his communication will still mark the context as collaborative, but at the metacommunication level he will reveal that the context has completely changed. In such cases the problem of deciphering the interactive context creates confusion, and stands in the way of learning and change.[3]

Faced with demands for denied coalitions, in short, the psychologist must not only decline to enter into them, but actively try to foil them. This type of intervention can rightly be called preventive.

PREVENTIVE ACTIONS OPEN TO THE PSYCHOLOGIST

Let us sum up what preventive actions involve:

- Respecting hierarchic channels in defining relationships.

- Circulating information.

- Actively searching for alliances.

Circulating information makes it clear from the outset what contacts the psychologist is trying to establish. If his respect for hierarchic levels does not include formal communications about his operations, he will have failed to forestall possible requests for a coalition, or suspicions that he is an "ally of" or a "plotter against." If, while defining his relationship with the heads of an organization, he were to meet the vice-president before the president, without explaining that this sequence was part of a clearly defined program of meetings, it might be misinterpreted. Take the case of our school system. As part of his original strategy, the psychologist, after meeting the director, asked to meet the chairman of the parents' association, with the nondeclared intention of defining the relationship between his team and the parents. He made it a special point to inform the director, who might otherwise have considered the meeting with the chairman a coalition against him.

Circulating information is a form of prevention on another level as well: it allows the psychologist to refuse offers of coalition, but without having to denigrate them. The psychologist, in fact, defines himself as an ally seeking a solution to a problem, someone who pays careful attention to the opinions of all, regardless of their role. This lays the foundation for relationships based on alliances. Psychologists working in organizations must cultivate alliances, lest they become isolated and ineffective.

We speak of an alliance when two or more persons define their relationship on the basis of a shared objective. That objective must be clear and obvious to all, and the relationship must be explicit. Moreover, the alliance must be open to all members of the organization with the same basic aspirations. An alliance must therefore be structured so that the members' attitudes to events or problems are explicit. In the case of the psychologist, that means defining contents, making concrete propositions, structuring projects, unifying the members of the organization. A model alliance of this type was forged by our psychologist when he made concrete proposals for putting on a puppet show (see Chapter 4). Here, of course, the path was that of analogic communication, rather than verbal pronouncements about the cold war that was being waged at the time.

A passive, wait-and-see attitude, based on the conviction that the psychologist must stay above the fray, is inappropriate in an organization: the psychologist would risk complete isolation.

Another danger to avoid is the ossification of alliances. An alliance is a relationship defined by precise contexts, limited in time. It must not be allowed to become perpetually fixed. It must be terminated as soon as the circumstances that gave rise to it have ceased to exist. Nothing must stop the psychologist, once a situation or the nature of certain problems has altered, from changing his system of alliances.

TOWARDS THE CONCEPT OF ORGANIZED COMPLEXITY

INTERACTIONAL COMPLEXITY AND COMMUNICATION | 9

CARLO RICCI

BEYOND THE DYAD

At least three interconnected factors lead to *interactional complexity* in a system:

- The number of parts, components, or players.

- The nature of the interdependence among them.

- The amount of uncertainty affecting their behavior.

Interactional complexity has not received enough attention, even from those who claim to use the systems model. Many theoretical statements pay lip service to the importance of viewing the system as a whole, no matter how complex, but very few methods have been developed to analyze complex interactional processes within systems.

Even the first factor, the number of players, intuitively so obvious, has too often been underrated. Any review of the literature shows that the dyadic model is the one most often used. But adding only one component (or player) to any system increases the complexity geometrically, rather than arithmetically.

It thus becomes necessary to study the relationships of relationships. Even the simple transition from analyzing the dyad ($N = 2$) to the triad ($N = 3$) can also be considered a qualitative jump requiring different methods of observation and analysis. For example, it is an oversimplification to use a dyadic sender-receiver paradigm in order to analyze the communication of one couple. In fact, in so doing, we obtain only an isolated description of that couple's exchange of messages. This does not mean that the dyad per se does not exist. We might work on this level, depending on our purpose and situation, *but only after an accurate exploration of a higher level of complexity.* One problem inherent in the dyadic model is that it does not consider many variables that affect communication. For instance, it excludes the entire *extended system of communication*—all the other people or groups who are involved with that dyadic relationship and influence it. But if we try to apply the dyadic model when we expand our observation to the N-adic communication system, we risk partitioning the system. The entire system would be reduced to the sum of the dyads, and so lose the interactional complexity of the N-person game. The analysis of interpersonal communication should be not dyadic but N-adic. The limitations of a dyadic model are apparent. The model itself tends to blur the extreme complexity of any communication process. Furthermore, the Cartesian assumption that the most complex can be explained in the terms of the simplest may lead to serious errors if applied to interpersonal communication. The systems approach demands the opposite assumption—that it is the most complex that explains the simplest. Thus a communicating dyad is inevitably part of a broader extended system of communication with a generally undefined number of participants. Any communication can be analyzed accurately only when the degree of complexity generated by the extended system is part of the analysis.

Take a certain three-person game ($N = 3$). The communication of the three participants cannot be explained by using a dyadic communication model ($N = 2$), because it is less complex than the ongoing game. At the higher degree of complexity ($N = 3$), new qualitative features become possible—for instance, coalitions (two against one, etc.), which are not possible in a two-person game.

Our first problem is assessing the exact size of the N-person game. In so doing, we define the boundaries of the extended system. It is very hard, often impossible, to define those boundaries; nevertheless, to go beyond the dyadic analysis of complex interaction, we need N-adic models of communication.

THE MODEL

As a starting point, let us consider the model of interpersonal communication suggested by Watzlawick, Beavin, and Jackson in *Pragmatics of Human Communication* (1967). From this model we know that "one cannot *not* communicate" (Axiom 1) and that any interpersonal communication implies a commitment between two people. Nevertheless, from our point of view, the receiver remains, for the most part, inadequately defined. An accurate definition of the receiver is needed if we are to understand the meaning of the sender's communication and the nature of his or her commitment. Too often the receiver is seen simply as the person who appears to be the person addressed. But by focusing on the two who appear to be the main communicators (the apparent source and receiver), we risk slipping into dyadic analysis.

Since a dyad may be studied within an N-adic communication system, every communication, even to just one receiver (the *apparent* one), inevitably commits the sender to the ongoing N-person game. *Therefore, the game itself, and not the various players, should be considered the real receiver of the sender's communication.* In terms of transmitting and receiving information, Haley's (1959) classic schema

1. I (sender)

2. am saying something (message)

3. to you (receiver)

4. in this situation (context)

can be modified as follows:

1. I (sender)

2. am saying something (message)

3. to you (apparent receiver)
   and inevitably and concomitantly

4. to him/them (other receiver[s])

5. in this situation (context)

With the above schema, it would clearly be a simplification to think of each communication as a private event between the two apparent communicators. It would be tantamount to accepting the hypothesis that each dyad (or part) enjoys perfect independence, and to ignoring the many relationships between the different parts and between each part and the whole.

It follows that the first axiom of the pragmatics of human communication could be reformulated as follows: *One cannot not play the ongoing N-person game.*

THE PARAMETERS OF COMMUNICATION

Field

The second axiom of communication posits that every communication has a *content* aspect, which we shall call X, as well as a *relationship* aspect, which we shall call Y. Hence we can represent the sender's communication (C) by

$$C = (X, Y)$$

where X indicates the content and Y the relationship between the communicators. However, that notation does not reflect the need to define the receiver of the communication. So we must add one more parameter to the above formula: the number of the participants in the ongoing game, which we shall call its *field* (N):

$$C = (X, Y, N)$$

Thus every communication has its own field (N) reflecting the many links by which the sender defines his relationship with all other players in the N-person game. When the field is not defined by the players, the game remains ambiguous, and the communication may seem irrational: the players may accuse one another of being illogical, even crazy. In fact, what makes a communication "rational" at a certain value of N may make it irrational at another.

A case in point is the president of the large company (Chapter 1) who lured a highly qualified expert away from a competitor to reorganize the purchasing department. One of the president's ploys was to invite him to several very confidential meetings. Yet when the expert settled into his new job, the president's behavior suddenly changed. He neither welcomed him nor introduced him to other managers, but very formally sent him to the head of the personnel department. Later, he made himself unavailable for several days, even by telephone. If the president's behavior is interpreted in purely dyadic terms, it seems irrational, inconsistent, and rude. But if we also include the vice-president in our observation, expanding the field from $N = 2$ to $N = 3$, the president's behavior looks different: since the vice-president was reluctant to accept any innovations, the president's coolness towards the expert served the "rational" purpose of reassuring the vice-president. From the point of view of the new department head, the president's distance after their previous confidential chats may have seemed inexplicable, even cruel; he could hardly be expected to understand it as an attempt to balance an interactional game that included the vice-president and other employees.

The concept of field (N), as we use it, is different from that of a group. Thus, if the sender is a family member, the field (N) of his communication (C) can be any number—greater or smaller than or equal to the number of the members of the family group. It follows that the clarification of the field of the communicators is an important step in analyzing interpersonal communication. Field is important in every communication, particularly if we consider that it may vary in time, may change according to content (X), and may remain ambiguous even to the communicators. It may happen that the sender, the apparent receiver, and the co-receivers (for example, the rest of the family) all define N differently. Consequently, each member may strike the others as irrational.

Furthermore, each player in the game may perceive the sender's field differently. Nevertheless, we assume that every communication has an N-value within which the sender's apparently irrational messages make sense.

Adopting the concept of field (N), we find that interactional complexity increases. At this point we should reconsider how the relationships (Y) among the N-players are defined.

To describe this aspect of communication, Watzlawick, Beavin, and Jackson (1967) formulated the axiom "All communication interchanges are either symmetrical or complementary depending on whether they are based on equality or difference." The complementary relationship assumes two different positions: "One partner occupies what has been variously described as the superior, primary, or 'one-up' position, and the other the corresponding inferior, secondary, or 'one-down' position. By contrast, the symmetric relationship is characterized by the 'minimization of difference.' "

The concept of field goes beyond dyadic descriptions by also considering the relation of the sender to all other players in the game. The relational structures increase exponentially with the increasing N-value of the field. If $N = 3$, the positions assumed by the interacting players can be described diagramatically. Figure 8a depicts a relational structure of equality in a triad. Figure 8b reflects the greatest diversity. Figures 8c and 8d depict mixed structures with two levels, and Figure 8e depicts a so-called "staff-line" structure in which one component of the triad plays the part of "consultant." By changing the positions of the three "players" in these five diagrams, which are really mini-organizational charts, we can obtain nineteen different triadic relational structures.

In the diagram the letters F, M, and S represent father, mother, and son, in a three-person game. Let us imagine the mother entering her son's bedroom early in the morning and saying, "It's seven o'clock." Obviously these words would be accompanied by different nonverbal expressions. From what has been said previously regarding territoriality, we can conclude from this message that the mother defines her position in relation not only to her son, but also to the father. The relationship between the father and the son must also be considered. *It should be noted that the father need not be present at the time of the communication in an ongoing three-person game.*

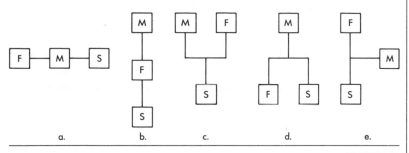

FIGURE 8.

The five diagrams depict relationships defined by the mother. We give each diagram a phrase reflecting the relational structure within the triad:

- Figure 8a: "The three of us agree that it's time to get up."

- Figure 8b: "I'm not like your father, who'd let you sleep till ten. Get up!"

- Figure 8c: "Your father and I have decided that it's high time you got up."

- Figure 8d: "You're a slacker like your father. If I weren't here to get you up . . ."

- Figure 8e: "Since your father has decided to take you out, I suppose it's time you got up."

These examples obviously do not cover all of the nineteen triadic relational structures the mother might define. Thus, if we placed the son on the same level as the father in Figure 8c, the mother might well say, "I'm only doing what you and your father have decided."

At this stage it should be clear that the effects of triadic communications (as in the examples above) on the apparent receiver may vary according to the receiver's view of the triad's organization.

In the situation represented in Figure 8d, the son might

refuse to get up, not because he disagreed that it was time or questioned his mother's right to call him, but because he disagreed with his mother's definition of his father. The son's behavior can be understood only if the observation goes beyond the dyadic level.

Since the relational aspects of a communication that go beyond the apparent sender-receiver dyad are generally conveyed nonverbally, the intended meaning is frequently ambiguous and may cause conflicts that are difficult to resolve. The son may agree with the content (having to get up at seven) and also with the mother's definition of herself in her relationship with him—but he may disagree with the mother's definition of her superiority over the father, whom she has placed on the son's level. It is possible that all these relational aspects beyond the mother-son dyad may define the area of the son's disagreement with the mother, and this could influence his behavior and provoke misunderstandings. Hence, considering the triadic nature of communication in a three-person game, the son, irrespective of his decision to stay in bed or get up, will inevitably become involved in the (probably implicit) conflict between the parents. His responses, regardless of his level of consciousness, are grounded in the triad and must be considered as a "move" in the ongoing N-person game—a move that will inevitably define him in respect to the parents.

At this point, it is not necessary to consider all the possible structures and conflicts in three-person games. It is quite enough to show that the change from a dyadic analysis to a triadic one exponentially increases the number of relationships that must be considered. The number and the quality of possible conflicts increase proportionately with the interactional complexity of the N-person game. This confirms the need to develop N-adic models of communication with which to try to match the interactional complexity of the N-person game.

Time

Another aspect of interpersonal communication that has not received enough attention is time (T). As with X (content), Y (relationship), and N (field), it is possible to qualify every communication differently according to the value of the time (T) within which the other variables occur. Hence, interpersonal communications can be represented by:

$$C = (X, Y, N, T)$$

Like field, time is a parameter that usually remains undefined. It may happen that the players in the N-person game communicate according to different time values (short, medium, and long). If these differences are ignored, communications may seem irrational, causing ambiguity and mutual accusations. Indeed, it is possible to prove that the qualities that make a communication seem "rational" on a short-term time scale may be contrary to those that would make it seem rational on another time scale.

It follows that although an agreement may by reached on X, Y, and N, it may be undermined by a discrepancy in the value of T. For example, in an organization, several people decided to form a research group, all agreeing that the group should be led by a certain member. In the final phase, though, the project was unexpectedly opposed by one member; the rationale of his objection remained unclear, which made him appear to be unreasonable. In due course, it emerged that he was not against the content of the project (X), or the leader and other organizational aspects (Y), or the composition of the group (N), but only against the ambiguous parameter of time (T). In fact, although he was prepared to accept X and N for a long time, he was not willing to accept the leader (Y) indefinitely.

In short, the expression

$$C = (X, Y, N, T)$$

makes it clear that for every communication at a given moment the players must clarify the field (N), the time (T), the content (X), and the relational aspects (Y), thereby clearly committing themselves to the ongoing game. It is thus possible to interpret each communication as a move in the N-person game.

The above formula enables us to describe every communication by means of the same "units of measurement" as are generally used in describing other basic concepts of organizations—for example, the concept of role. In fact, as the parameters X, Y, N, and T may define the communication itself, they are equally capable of defining "role." A role may be defined as the sum total of information specifying such aspects as what to do (X); how to do it (Y)—that is, how to relate effectively to the roles of other players;

the number of players with whom one must make contact (*N*); the relevant time span (*T*).

By means of the formula, we can relate communication to role. This may be an antidote against the analytical tendency to compartmentalize the aspects of such complex processes as interpersonal communication. Similarly, the formula may be useful in analyzing communications in large organizations.

Duality

Every communication is characterized by the way the four parameters *(X, Y, N, T)* are combined. All possible combinations constitute the complete universe of communications, and a particular combination represents a selection from a universe of communications. It follows that *every communication involves a selection among alternatives, in the sense that other communications have been excluded.* Irrespective of how consciously it is made, *every* communication has meaning with respect to the ongoing game; "not saying or doing anything" is a communication full of meaning, if only by virtue of what has been excluded in the making of that choice. From these statements there emerges an important property of communication, namely *duality.* If we add the simultaneous inclusion-exclusion phenomenon, the interactional complexity of any communication increases.

In general, the attribution of meaning is usually derived from a single aspect: from what has been communicated by a certain choice of *X, Y, N, T.* Nevertheless, it is also possible to refer to what has been excluded. No problem arises when the choice of the communication is made from a universe of two possibilities; what has been chosen fully conveys what has been rejected, and vice versa.

But confusion may arise when the choice is made from a universe with more than two possibilities. For example, an adolescent boy is encouraged by his parents to take up sports. He takes up a sport, trains ardently, and eventually becomes a champion in his league. At this stage, his parents unexpectedly disapprove. It is hard for him to realize that his parents' original encouragement had nothing to do with the merit of sports as such, but only with the dangers it was believed to avert (bad company, masturbation, drugs, etc.), and they now see other dangers in his too-active participation.

Duality is a property of communication that may dramatically increase interactional complexity and that may also hamper the study of interactional behavior.

Interpersonal communication must be considered an extremely complex phenomenon in which different "levels of reality" are simultaneously present. The levels described above by no means exhaust the many dimensions of human communication, but they are a first step in developing N-adic models of communication that try to match the interactional complexity of N-person games. Hence, if we agree that communication is inevitably a move to place oneself in relation to other players in the ongoing N-person game, then every communication should be judged as a complex operation through which all the "levels of reality" that characterize the N-person game become integrated and synthesized. The different "levels of reality" may meet in every communication, remaining distinct or blending together, and produce a kind of harmony in spite of their contradictions—or else their incompatibility may turn them into an explosive mixture.

NOTES

References in notes are to works listed in the Bibliography.

PREFACE

1.   Bateson, 1978, p.87.

1   A Psychologist in Industry

1.   In this connection, Anna Anfossi writes that organizations may undergo structural developments in the wake of which the distinctions between managerial categories are blurred to the point of merging at the middle- and junior-management levels. This explains why managerial participation in the decision-making process becomes a mere sham, giving rise to acute dissatisfaction and to the "identity crisis" of many middle-management sectors who are at two different levels of the organizational chart (an upper decision-making level, and a lower functional level) and are unable to fit psychologically into either. Many managers are nowadays deeply shaken by that identity crisis, with consequent frustrations and anxieties. Essentially, the process downgrades their functional status, but with no effect on their salaries, which have become a means of "buying the loyalty" of these frustrated strata (Anfossi, 1978, p.330). This observation seems particularly applicable to the company examined here.

In organizations of the traditional type, there is a proliferation of hierarchic levels holding real, as well as symbolic, power. This extension and reinforcement of the hierarchic structure "by the decentralization of decisions has a double aim: choosing managers who bear responsibility in the hierarchy and persuading them to identify themselves with the company in such a way as to increase their loyalty and thus strengthen company control over those excluded from the hierarchy. The success of such operations depends not only on the reaction of the various sectors of the company but also and above all on its promise of economic security. It is a costly and often disappointing operation that often culminates in gigantic hierarchic structures and the multiplication of controls beyond any functional necessity. The number of discontented people deprived of any real power exceeds the number of satisfied people; discipline, in its traditional sense, rarely guarantees the necessary efficiency, already undermined by the cost of the operation." To some extent D. Anfossi's theory is also applicable to the situation in the In-Service Training Center (described in Chapter 2).

On the subject of the relationship between top management and hierarchy, Likert (1961) has described four types of chain of command: authoritarian, paternalistic, consultative, and participatory, and argues that the last is the most efficient. Organizations of the traditional type can develop towards "flexible coordination," i.e., are capable of adapting continually to new situations, much like systems capable of self-regulation under dynamic conditions (Haberstroh, 1965).

2.   Repetitive situations, apart from their sterility, tend towards maximum entropy and growth of homeostatic mechanisms. Development, by contrast, is characterized by a rapid flow of information and an exchange of energy between the system and its environment.

Flexibility, the ability to adapt to new conditions, is one of the basic features of functional systems. Another is innovation, which presupposes a capacity not only for adaptation but also for the "creation" of new situations (Anfossi, 1978, p.237). In economics, Schumpeter (1943) has shown that in situations of "circular flow," the productive process becomes a continual repetition of the same decisions. The result is a situation without risks or uncertainties, but also without profit. According to Schumpeter, innovation alone is the basis of dynamic developments whose reward is profit.

Our company, as we saw, gave pride of place to the technical and executive sector and to the staff of superspecialists. (The explanation for this attitude will be found in Chapter 5.) The immediate object was to build up the myth of a model enterprise facing the winds of change with all the advantages. It is important to remember that, at the time, the fusion of research and development with economic and financial policy was in great vogue. More recent studies have demonstrated the advantages of an interdisciplinary approach, involving the economic, psychological, and sociological sectors, and have revealed the importance of cybernetic organization.

In this connection let us recall that the interdisciplinary approach is one of the cornerstones of systems theory. As Durand (1979) has put it, systems need many different elements to survive: "Living, natural systems have a higher diversity than they strictly need; they thus have a reserve of variety that enables them, in the event of one of their elements or vital circuits breaking down, to fall back on another element or reserve circuit" (p.21). This is also what is needed in organizations created by man. Jacques Mélèse in his *L'analyse modulaire des systèmes* (1972) has drawn attention to the need for specific variety in business. He maintains that organizations lacking adequate variety are threatened by excessive complications and by bureaucratic sclerosis.

3. It was probably for that very reason that the company did not bring in an external consultant but took on a full-time industrial psychologist. It obviously did not seem prudent to wash the company's dirty linen in public.

2 A Psychologist in a Research Center

1. All the names used here are, of course, fictitious.

3 Two Psychologists in a Pediatrics Ward

1. Though the traditional approach in social research favors laboratory experiments, it also sanctions the study of phenomena in the social context in which they occur. Such studies, however, tend to isolate the research group and its work from the environment in which the research takes place. This is true of the "method of participant observation," in which the research worker is considered part of the social context that is the object of his inquiry. However, with the traditional approach, the researcher must be careful not to alter the situation he studies by his very presence. To that end, he must either disguise his role of observer by merging with the object of his research or, where that is impossible, reduce his involvement as much as he possibly can (cf. B. S. Phillips, 1971, pp.229–44; and R. Dahrendorf, 1965).

The advocates of the traditional methodological model did, in fact, believe that they could overcome the problem of the relationship between the observing and the observed systems by focusing attention on conditions that reduce the interactions between the two. In this view, the laboratory in particular, with its many restrictions, is considered the ideal background for social research, inasmuch as it creates the optimum distance between the observer and the system he observes.

As everyone knows, however, this methodological model now stands on very shaky ground, its critics having shown that even laboratory research cannot ignore the context in which it takes place. Thus, R. Rosenthal and M. T. Orne in exemplary studies have demonstrated that experimental subjects tend to respond in accordance with what they believe to be "experimenter expectancy." Experimenters unconsciously convey the way in which they would like the subjects to respond (M. T. Orne and L. A. Gustafson, 1965; and R. Rosenthal et al., 1966). R. Harré and P. F. Secord (1972) have gone even further by asserting that the traditional form of experimental psychology can be considered a particular type of social relationship, namely, that of interactions between strangers, and that the rules determining the behavior of experimental psychologists and their subjects can be seen as very similar to those governing the encounters of strangers. Harré and Secord have suggested an alternative methodological model in which the significance attached by the psychologist or the subject to the experimental situation is considered an integral part of the experiment.

Harré and Secord's study is just one of many examples of recent interest in the research context. However, none of the many writers concerned has yet been able to show fully how these contextual variables can be turned to good effect in research work.

2.   See J. Bowlby (1969 and 1973) for the explicit theoretical assumptions of the research group led by Bowlby. Their theoretical reference model was based on a combination of psychoanalytical and theological concepts. See also J. Bowlby, M. Ainsworth, M. Boston, and D. Rosenbluth (1956); J. Robertson and D. Rosenbluth (1952); J. Robertson (1973); J. Robertson (1968).

3.   For a critical analysis of the "maternal deprivation" concept, see M. Rutter (1972). The ideological implications of the concept have been examined by J. Mitchell (1974). For the restrictions placed on research into child hospitalization by Bowlby and Robertson's approach, see M. Stacey (1976), and D. Hall and M. Stacey (1979).

4.   J. Haley, 1963, p.11.

5.   P. Watzlawick, J. H. Beavin, and D. D. Jackson, 1967, p.67. For a deeper discussion of the concept of schismogenesis see G. Bateson (1936 and 1972).

6.   Oddly enough, the former chief physician, priding himself on the fact that the new chief was his "heir," continued for quite some time to appear in the department and also to attend the Friday meetings. This form of behavior was certainly not designed to make the new chief feel more at home in the department.

7.   It must be pointed out that the psychologists found it impossible to convene meetings that could be attended by the entire nursing staff (in contrast to the doctors) since the nurses worked in shifts.

4   A Team of Educational Psychologists in a Suburban School District

1.   In this connection we should like to draw attention to what Schein (1969) calls "process consultation." By that term he refers to a consultant's efforts to make his client look at events as part of a process in the client's environment and to act accordingly. The consultant's role, in that approach, is not to tackle the problem himself but to teach the client how to diagnose and cure it. In other words, the client must be actively involved in the formulation of the solution. If the client is an organization, the consultant must pay particular attention to the way the organization approaches him. He should carefully note who makes the first contact with him and through what channels.

Schein also attaches great importance to the exploratory meeting that follows and to the persons who participate in it. He mentions several criteria for deciding who should be invited to, and who excluded from, the exploratory meeting. Those invited should include: someone in fairly high authority who can help influence the rest, especially if he is in favor of process consultation; someone who agrees with the idea of engaging a consultant for specific ends; someone who has defined specific problems to be tackled; and someone familiar with the concept of process consultation. By contrast, hostile persons and anyone totally ignorant of the consultant's potential contribution should be excluded.

Schein specifies how long the first meeting should last, and that it must be paid for, since the consultation process starts with the first contact.

Schein stresses that the consultant must make it perfectly clear to his clients what he does and does not intend to do. He must also be clear about the fact that his client is the entire group with which he is about to work—the entire organization and not just the person who has made contact with him. He must define the framework in which he will operate, establish a timetable, and define his working method and objectives. Process consultation proper does not start until the potential client has accepted the fact that relationships and interpersonal processes are important subjects of investigation: the client's readiness to submit to observation and research is, according to Schein, a prerequisite of a successful consultative relationship. Schein insists further that the psychologist have no predetermined solutions or *ad hoc* recipes, and that he must be ready to engage in dialogue. Schein stresses that each step in process consultation constitutes an intervention. This is true even of the initial act, the decision to work with a given organization. It follows that the consultant must assess his every step in the light of its possible effects on the organization; i.e., he must base his actions on the realization that his behavior as a whole constitutes a kind of intervention. This is true even of the way in which he elicits information.

Despite the many similarities between Schein's method and that used by our psychologist, there are some fundamental differences in approach. Schein proposes to exclude hostile persons, at least during the first meeting, but our experience has taught us that to do so is a grave mistake, since the hostile subjects often grow even more hostile and build a defensive wall around themselves. It is also worth recalling that there is a profound difference between a consultation paid for directly by the organization client and one paid for by a different system, for instance by a local authority responsible for a school system.

2.   The concept of "totality" as used by Gestalt psychologists has been developed by K. Lewin, who introduced the concepts of the "group as a dynamic whole" and of "quasi-stationary equilibrium." With Lewin, psychologists began to consider phenomena in the setting in which they occur. They thus advanced from the Aristotelian approach to a dynamic conception of the interaction between individuals, and between individuals and their environment, the stress being laid on the relationship between elements and the whole of which they are a part. General systems theory has developed that concept even further. Thus, von Bertalanffy has shown that a system is an irreducible whole. The fundamental concepts of systems theory are interaction, totality, organization, and complexity. Among the many definitions of systems, special mention should be made of that of the great linguist and pioneer Ferdinand de Saussure (1959): "A system is an organized whole made up of interdependent elements that can be defined only with reference to each other and in terms of their positions in the whole."

3.   A recent Italian law grants the elected chairman of the school board the right to intervene in decisions made by the school administration.

4.   During this period the group first came across the writings of D. G. Livingston (1977), which we recommend to the reader's attention because the

author outlines a very shrewd strategy for dealing with open conflicts between various sections of an organization. We believe that such conflict situations can give rise to repetitive games capable of reducing learning potential to near zero levels (inability to correct mistakes by trial and error). Livingston has shown how a conflict between two openly hostile groups can be handled effectively. To that end, he has framed the following basic rules:

- Mind your own business and let others mind theirs.

- Speak of the present, i.e., remain solidly anchored in the *here and now.*

Livingston believes that all meetings must have a fixed beginning and end. Moreover, meetings will go on endlessly and pointlessly if people engage in recriminations about the past and keep laying down what others should not be doing.

5. Anyone making important changes is likely to commit errors, which he must be prepared to remedy at some cost to himself (Likert, 1961). That cost need not necessarily be a bad thing—it may, in fact, be the price for deeper understanding. As Kurt Lewin has put it, "If you want to understand something, try to change it."

"Every deficiency or dysfunction in information imposes a cost, often precisely measurable, on the system" (Anfossi, 1978, p.320). In our case, the psychologist's mistake threatened to undermine the relationship between himself and the teachers, but the information it yielded—that one must always abstain from creating evaluative contexts—was of great importance.

5 The Organization Plays a Game of Its Own

1. In J. Boszormenyi-Nagy and J. Framo, 1965, p.413.
2. In systemic research, every step brings home the difficulty of mastering the complexities involved. Often, one feels ashamed not to have understood what seems perfectly obvious in retrospect. The fact that this still happens to us after years of special training underlines the substantial unity of the metasystem made up of the observer and the observed system. E. Morin has suggested a methodological solution: "Let the observer observe himself even while observing the system, and let him try to understand his own understanding" (1977, p.143). In practice, experience has repeatedly taught me that a fairly long interval is needed before one can reach a metalevel. Situations that seem inextricable and confused "in the hot state" prove easily decipherable "in the cold." Sometimes our basic error does not strike us until months after the end of the treatment. It is as if "understanding" needs the prolonged separation of the two systems (observer and observed). This fact unfortunately not only prolongs the research but also constitutes an obstacle to timely interventions.
3. This conception is not entirely alien to psychosociology, and was first put forward by students of organizational development. "Organizations are open systems placed in an unstable environment" (Schein, 1969). The concept of "environmental turbulence," and two other concepts (the surmounting of bureaucracy and the inevitability of democracy), are central to the theoretical armory

of organization development. Its aim is the study of general observational systems within a permanently developing society subject to constant, rapid, and unexpected changes in an unstable environment. That is why organizations must cope with the turbulence of the social environment if they are to survive.

The leading exponents of organizational development are Argyris, Bennis, Beckhard, Blake, Muton, and Schein. They believe that the past few decades have been characterized by "deflagrations" in the wake of radical changes in the values and objectives of social organizations. According to Stella and Quaglino (1976), it was Bennis and Beckhard, in particular, who first drew attention to some of the more important "explosions" whose effects are still making themselves felt: the explosion in education, in technology, in knowledge, the demographic explosion, the economic explosion, and the communications explosion.

The importance of organizations conceived as open systems in constant dynamic interaction with the environment has been stressed in numerous studies, summarized by Crozier and Friedberg (1977).

They have also drawn attention to the persistence of the "determinist" belief that the environment is a set of "impersonal" factors whose objective characteristics are stamped automatically and directly on organizations. The result is a unilateral view of the influence of the environment, which is, in fact, made up of a host of scattered fields with fluctuating, ambiguous, divergent, and often contradictory "demands."

Crozier and Friedberg have demonstrated the importance of the inevitable interference between the organizational system and its technical, economic, social, and cultural context. This explains the difficulty in, indeed the impossibility of, drawing a clear line between what is "internal" and what is "external." In 1961, Burns and Stalker posed the problem of the integration of organizational structures in their environment and the level of their adaptation. They went on to identify specific models of organization corresponding to various socioeconomic environments.

Emery and Trist (1965) have examined causal interrelations between external elements and the structure of an organization. Their Taylorist view of an organization as a mechanical set of cogs with a rationality of its own has been superseded by Crozier and Friedberg's view that an organization is a conflictual universe functioning as a result of the collision of the contingent, multiple, and divergent rationalities of relatively free actors using whatever source of power is at their disposal. According to these authors, "An organization does not exist *because* but *in spite* of the action of its members."

A more optimistic and detached, and hence more systemic, view of the individual has been given by Schein (1965). He contends, "If we grant that every system has a variety of functions, and assume that it exists in an environment likely to add unpredictable elements, then the efficiency of a system can be defined as its capacity for survival, adaptation, self-preservation, and for developing independently of its particular functions." By particular functions he refers to the variety of functions and objectives the system fulfills, even if these are self-contradictory. There has thus been an advance from the old view that an organization is effective if it satisfies one of the following three criteria: high productivity, high staff morale, efficient service. At the systemic level, the efficiency criterion must be capable of being extended to a much wider range of factors. It follows that the view of organizations as closed systems moving in a universe of their own in which they are constantly threatened with explosions is outdated. An organization poses a set of problems whose solution is not easy, and whose nature must be accurately identified by anyone anxious to help it survive. The systemic view of organizations has the advantage of focusing attention on many problems that have remained opaque to the older theories and mechanistic models. It seems possible to conclude that the ever-growing instability of the environment, the constant external pressures, and the complexity of relations between organizations and the environment make it essential to adopt a systemic approach to the problem.

6 The Psychologist Must Consider His Own Role

1.   In his discussion of "social consultation," Sofer (1961) has made an indepth study of the effects an observer can have on the environment he is about to analyze, and also on the way in which he can use those effects to enlarge his understanding of what happens around him. He makes a clear distinction between the process of collecting data and discussing them with those members of the organization who have supplied them, so as to drive home the relationship between the variables. Rice (1963), on the other hand, thinks of himself as a measuring instrument and suggests that the psychologist's analyses of his own feelings of pleasure and anguish, anxiety and relief, agitation and self-control are the best criteria for distinguishing between what is real and what is not real. In this connection we may well ask with Watzlawick (1976) if reality is indeed real. Rice believes that an analysis of the psychologist's attitude and feelings towards his client, and vice versa, helps to focus attention on the problem under discussion. The decision to bring in an outside consultant, according to Rice, may be due to a real problem the organization is unable to solve. But there can be other, latent difficulties of which the problem is merely a symptom. In that case, the solution of the manifest problem not only will prove ineffective, but can even increase the latent difficulties.

Rice puts forward three methods of satisfying contradictory demands: namely, devoting oneself exclusively to the solution of the manifest problem while bearing in mind the latent problem but not mentioning it explicitly, tackling the problem on both levels, and ignoring the manifest problem the better to tackle the latent problem. He bases his choice of one of these three methods on the evaluation of a number of factors. Thus, if he notices during the consultation that he has contradictory feelings such as anxiety or embarrassment or satisfaction, he examines these feelings and tries to determine which spring from him and which from the consultant-client relationship. Once he has "made sure" that the second is the case, he can go on to consider himself a ready measuring instrument. Rice also pays careful attention to his personal involvement with the client, because he believes that it is a measure of the client's involvement with him and also facilitates access to the necessary data. Rice attaches fundamental importance to the analysis of transferential feelings about their relationship and about reality. With the systemic approach, by contrast, it is essential not to allow oneself to become entangled in personal relationships, so as to avoid the risk of confusing logical levels: "The causes, the question why, and emotions must stay in the black box" (Selvini et al., 1975). Nor is that all. There is also the problem of what criteria (or models) the psychologist can use to distinguish with certainty whether his feelings at a given moment spring from the relationship with his client, or from elements of his own personality. We know perfectly well that the elements of the psychologist's personality, too, have a relational origin. Hence, rather than pretend, as Rice suggests, that he can discern the indiscernible, the psychologist would do better to focus attention on the "main" relational models he has acquired in the course of his experience and which he tends to repeat (however vaguely) in certain situations.

2. Bateson, 1973, pp.250ff.

3. The lecture ("Social Planning and the Concept of Deutero-Learning") is collected in Bateson, 1973; see pp.133ff. This concept is similar to that of learning sets suggested by Harlow (1949) in his work on the training of rhesus monkeys. As a result of training, these animals become more and more capable of solving discriminated learning problems of increasing difficulty; that is, they learn to learn By means of appropriate exercises it is possible to teach monkeys to perform very complex tasks; for example, to choose an odd object from a set, or to choose an object to match one presented by the experimenter.

7 The Psychologist and the Problem of Hierarchic Levels

1. Selvini et al., 1978.

2. For the distinction between the content and the relationship levels of communication, see Bateson (1951, pp.179–81); and Watzlawick, Beavin, and Jackson (1967, pp.51–54).

8 Denied Coalitions

1. Haley, 1967, pp.16–17.

2. Bateson, 1972, pp.297ff.

3. The confusion of, and changes in, contexts impede learning because they face the individual with several *sets* of alternatives from which he must make his next choice (see Bateson, 1972, p.260).

BIBLIOGRAPHY

Anfossi, A. *Prospettive sociologiche sull'organizzazione aziendale*. Milan: F. Angeli, 1978.

Argyris, C. *Intervention Theory and Method*. Reading, Mass.: Addison-Wesley, 1970.

Argyris, C. *The Applicability of Organizational Sociology*. Cambridge, Mass.: Harvard University Press, 1972.

Argyris, C. & D. Schon. *Theory in Practice: Increasing Professional Effectiveness*. San Francisco: Yossy Bass, 1974.

Argyris, C. *Increasing Leadership Effectiveness*. New York: Wiley, 1976.

Ashby, W. R. *Design for a Brain*. London: Chapman & Hall, 1952.

Ashby, W. R. *An Introduction to Cybernetics*. London: Chapman & Hall, 1956.

Ashby, W. R. "Principles of the Self-Organizing System." In H. von Foerster & G. W. Zopf, eds. *Principles of Self-Organization*. New York: Pergamon, 1962.

Balle, C. & J. L. Peaucelle. *Le pouvoir informatique dans l'entreprise*. Paris: Ed. d'Organisation, 1972.

Bateson, G. *Naven*. Cambridge: Cambridge University Press, 1936.

Bateson, G. *Steps to an Ecology of Mind*. New York: Ballantine, 1972.

Bateson, G. *Mind and Nature*. New York: Dutton, 1978

Battacchi, M. W. Introduction to *L'indagine sperimentale in psicologia*, by R. Hyman. Milan: Martello, 1972.

Beckhard, R. *Organization Development: Strategies and Models.* Reading, Mass.: Addison-Wesley, 1969.

Beer, S. "Below the Twilight Arch." In *General Systems Yearbook,* 1960.

Bennis, W. G. *Changing Organizations: Essays on the Development and Evolution of Human Organization.* New York: McGraw-Hill, 1966.

Bennis, W. G. *Organization Development: Its Nature, Origins, and Prospects.* Reading, Mass.: Addison-Wesley, 1969.

Bertalanffy, L. von. *General System Theory: Foundations, Development, Applications.* Harmondsworth: Penguin, 1973.

Boguslaw, R. *The New Utopians.* Englewood Cliffs, N.J.: Prentice-Hall, 1965.

Boszormenyi-Nagy, J. & J. Framo, eds. *Intensive Family Therapy: Theoretical and Practical Aspects.* New York: Harper & Row, 1965.

Bowlby, J., J. Robertson & D. Rosenbluth. "A Two-Year-Old Goes to Hospital." *Psychoanalytic Study of the Child* 7(1952): 82–94.

Bowlby, J., M. Ainsworth, M. Boston & D. Rosenbluth. "The Effects of Mother Child Separation: A Follow-Up Study." *The British Journal of Medical Psychology* 3–4(1956): 211–47.

Bowlby, J. *Attachment and Loss.* London: Hogarth Press, 1969.

Buckley, W. *Sociology of Modern System Theory.* Englewood Cliffs, N.J.: Prentice-Hall, 1967.

Burns, T. & G. M. Stalker. *The Management of Innovation.* London: Tavistock, 1961.

Crozier, M. & E. Friedberg. *L'acteur et le système.* Paris: Ed. du Seuil, 1977.

Dahrendorf, R. *Sociologia dell'industria e dell'azienda.* Milan: Jaca, 1965.

Durand, D. *La Systémique.* Paris: Puff, 1979.

Emery, F. E. & E. L. Trist. "The Causal Texture of Organizational Environment." *Human Relations* 18(1965): 21–32.

Emery, F. E., ed. *Systems Thinking: Selected Readings.* Harmondsworth: Penguin, 1969.

Enriquez, E. "La notion du pouvoir." In P. Drioli, ed. *L'économie et les sciences humaines,* vol. 1. Paris: Dunod, 1967.

Enriquez, E. "Imaginaire social, refoulement et repression dans les organisations." *Connexions,* no. 3. Paris: Epi, 1972.

Enriquez, E. "Problematique du changement." *Connexions,* no. 4. Paris: Epi, 1972.

Etzioni, A. *Sociologia dell'organizzazione.* Bologna: Il Mulino, 1967.

Goldthorpe, J. H. "Social Stratification in Industrial Society." *Sociological Review,* Monograph 8.

Gouldner, A. W. *Organizational Analysis.* New York: Basic Books, 1959.

Gouldner, A. W. *Patterns of Industrial Bureaucracy.* Glencoe, Ill.: Free Press, 1954.

Gray, W., F. J. Duhl & N. D. Rizzo, eds. *General Systems Theory and Psychiatry.* Boston: Little-Brown, 1964.

Haberstroh, C. J. "Organization Design and Systems Analysis." In J. G. March. *Handbook of Organizations.* Chicago: Rand McNally, 1965.

Haire, M., ed. *Organization Theory in Industrial Practice: A Symposium.* Ann Arbor: Ann Arbor Foundation for Research on Human Behavior, 1959.

Haley, J. "The Family of the Schizophrenic: A Model System." *Journal of Nervous and Mental Diseases* 129(1959): 357–74. Also included in D. D. Jackson, ed. *Communication, Family, and Marriage*. Palo Alto: Science and Behavior Books, 1968.

Haley, J. *Strategies of Psychotherapy*. New York: Grune & Stratton, 1963.

Haley, J. "Towards a Theory of Pathological Systems." In G. M. Zuk & I. Boszormenyi-Nagy, eds. *Family Therapy and Disturbed Families*. Palo Alto, Calif.: Science and Behavior Books, 1967.

Hall, D. & M. Stacey, eds. *Beyond Separation: Further Studies of Children in Hospital*. London: Routledge & Kegan Paul, 1979.

Harlow, H. E. "The Nature of Learning Sets." *Psychol. Review* 56(1949): 51–65.

Harper, J., A. L. Scoresby & W. D. Boyce. "The Logical Level of Complementary, Symmetrical, and Parallel Interaction Classes in Family Dyads." *Family Process* 16(1977): 199–211.

Harré, R. & P. F. Secord. *La spiegazione del comportamento sociale*. Bologna: Il Mulino, 1977.

Heller, K. "Ambiguity in the Interview Interaction." In J. Shlien, ed. *Research in Psychotherapy*, vol. 3. Washington, D.C.: American Psychological Association, 1968.

Hildebrand, H. P. "Psychanalyse et institution." In *Atti del convegno internazionale psicoanalisi e istituzioni, Milano, 30 October 1976*. Florence: Le Monnier, 1978, 17–26.

Iberall, A., et al. *Progress Toward the Application of System Science Concepts to Biology*. Arlington, Va.: Army Research Office, 1972.

Jonson, R. A., F. E. Kast & J. E. Rosenzweig. *The Theory and Management of Systems*. New York: McGraw-Hill, 1967.

Katz, D. & R. L. Kahn. *The Social Psychology of Organizations*. New York: Wiley, 1966.

Kuhn, T. S. *The Structure of Scientific Revolutions*. Chicago: University of Chicago, 1962.

Laing, R. D. *The Self and Others: Further Studies in Sanity and Madness*. London: Tavistock, 1961.

Laing, R. D., H. Phillipson, & A. R. Lee. *Interpersonal Perception: A Theory and Method of Research*. New York: Springer, 1966.

Lawrence, P. R. & J. W. Lorsch. *Organization and Environment*. Cambridge, Mass.: Harvard Business School, 1967.

Lewin, C. *A Dynamic Theory of Personality*. New York & London: McGraw-Hill, 1935.

Lewin, C. *Resolving Social Conflicts: Selected Papers on Group Dynamics*. Edited by G. W. Lewin. Ann Arbor: University of Michigan Research Center for Group Dynamics, 1948.

Lewin, C. *Field Theory in Social Science: Selected Papers on Group Dynamics*. Edited by Dorwin Cartwright. Ann Arbor: University of Michigan Research Center for Group Dynamics, 1951.

Likert, R. *New Patterns of Management*. New York: McGraw-Hill, 1961.

Likert, R. *The Human Organization: Its Management and Value*. New York: McGraw-Hill, 1967.

Livingston, D. G. "Rules of the Road: Doing Something Simple About Conflict in the Organization. *Personnel,* February, 1977, 23–29.

Luhmann, N. *Potere e complessità sociale.* Milan: Il Saggiatore, 1979.

Maccacaro, G. M., ed. "Il bambino è dell'ospedale?" In Robertson, *Bambini in ospedale.* Milano: Feltrinelli, 1973.

March, J. G. & H. A. Simon, with Harold Guetzkow. *Organization.* New York: Wiley; London: Chapman & Hall, 1958.

McGregor, D. *The Human Side of Enterprise.* New York: McGraw-Hill, 1960.

Mélèse, J. *L'analyse modulaire des systèmes.* Paris: Hommes et Techniques, 1972.

Miller, J. G. *Living Systems.* New York: McGraw-Hill, 1978.

Minuchin, S. *Families of the Slums: An Exploration of Their Structure and Treatment.* New York: Basic Books, 1967.

Minuchin, S. *Families and Family Therapy.* Cambridge, Mass.: Harvard University Press, 1974.

Mitchell, Juliet. *Psychoanalysis and Feminism.* London: Allen Lane, 1974.

Monod, J. *Chance and Necessity.* London: Collins, 1972.

Morin, E. *La méthode, la nature de la nature.* Paris: Le Seuil, 1977.

Morin, E. *La vie de la vie.* Paris: Le Seuil, 1980.

Moscovici, S. *Society Against Nature,* 1972.

Moscovici, S. *Social Influences and Social Change.* London: Academic Press, 1976.

Orne, M. T. & L. A. Gustafson. "Effects of Perceived Role and Role Success on the Detection of Deception." *Journal of Applied Psychology* (1965): 412–17.

Parsons, T. *The Social System.* Glencoe, Ill.: Free Press, 1951.

Parsons, T. *Social Structure and Personality.* New York: Free Press of Glencoe; London: Collier-Macmillan, 1964.

Phillips, B. S. *Social Research: Strategy and Tactics,* 2nd ed. New York: Macmillan, 1971.

Prigogine, I. & J. M. Wiame. "Biologie et thermodynamique des phénomènes irréversibles." *Experientia* 2(1946): 451.

Prigogine, I., G. Nicolis, & A. Babloyantz. "Thermodynamics of Evolution." *Physics Today* 11(1972): 23; and 12(1972): 38.

Prigogine, I. "L'ordine per fluttuazione e la dinamica dei sistemi." In E. Agazzi, ed. *I sistemi tra scienza e filosofia.* Turin: SAI, 1978.

Rice, A. K. *The Enterprise and Its Environment: A System Theory of Management Organisation.* London: Tavistock, 1963.

Robertson, James. *Young Children in Hospital.* London: Tavistock, 1958.

Robertson, James. *Young Children in Hospital.* 2nd ed. London: Tavistock, 1970.

Robertson, James. *Hospitals and Children: A Parent's-Eye View.* London: Victor Gollancz, 1962.

Robertson, James. "The Longstay Child in Hospital." *Maternal Child Care* 4(1968): 161–6.

Rosenthal, R., et al. "Data Desirability, Experimenter Expectancy, and the Results of Pychological Research." *Journal of Personality and Social Psychology* 3(1966): 20–7.

de Rosnay, J. *Il macroscopio: Verso una visio globale.* Bari: Dedalo, 1978.

Rutter, M. *Maternal Deprivation Reassessed.* London: Penguin, 1972.
de Saussure, F. *Course in General Linguistics.* New York: Philosophical Library, 1959.
Schein, E. H. *Organizational Psychology.* Englewood Cliffs, N.J.: Prentice-Hall, 1965.
Schein, E. H. *Process Consultation: Its Role in Organization Development.* Reading, Mass.: Addison-Wesley, 1969.
Schumpeter, J. A. *Capitalism, Socialism and Democracy.* London: Allen & Unwin, 1943.
Selvini Palazzoli, M. "Lezioni dell'anno accademico 1978–79 presso l'Istituto di Psicologia dell'Università Cattolica." Unpublished ms.
Selvini Palazzoli, M., L. Boscolo, G. Cecchin & G. Prata. *Paradosso e contraparadosso.* Milano: Feltrinelli, 1975.
Selvini Palazzoli, M., et al. *Il mago smagato.* Milan: Feltrinelli, 1976.
Selvini Palazzoli, M., et al. "I trabocchetti delle istituzioni." *Terapia Familiare* 4(1978): 42–57.
Silverman, D. *The Theory of Organizations: A Sociological Framework.* London: Heinemann Educational, 1970.
Sluzki, C. E. & E. Vernon. "The Double Bind as a Universal Pathogenic Situation." *Family Process* 10(1971): 397–417.
Sofer, C. *The Organization from Within. A Comparative Study of Social Institutions Based on the Sociotherapeutic Approach.* London: Tavistock, 1961.
Stacey, M., ed. *Hospitals, Children, and Their Families. The Report of a Pilot Study.* London: Routledge & Kegan Paul, 1976.
Stella, S. & G. P. Quaglino. *Prospettive di psicosociologia.* Milan: F. Angeli, 1976.
Tajfel, H. "La psicologia sociale e i processi sociali." *Giornale italiana di psicologia* 3(1976): 189–221.
Toronto, R. S. "A General System Model for the Analysis of Organizational Change." *Behavioral Science* 5(1975): 145–160.
Toulmin, S. & J. Goodfield. *The Architecture of Matter.* New York: Harper & Row, 1962.
Watzlawick, P., J. H. Beavin & D. D. Jackson. *Pragmatics of Human Communication.* New York: Norton, 1967.
Watzlawick, P., J. H. Weakland & R. Fisch. *Change: Principles of Problem Formation and Problem Resolution.* New York: Norton, 1974.
Watzlawick, P. *How Real Is Real?* Englewood Cliffs, N.J.: Prentice-Hall, 1976.
Watzlawick, P. *The Language of Change.* New York: Basic Books, 1978.
Wynne, L. & C. Thaler Singer. "Thought Disorders and the Family Relations of Schizophrenics." *Arch. of Gen. Psychiatr.* 9(1963): 191–296; and 12(1965): 187–212.

INDEX

accommodation, 137
ad hoc group research, 113
aggression, 46, 47
agreement at any price, 50
alliances, 7, 12, 13, 41, 94–95,
    125
  alliances for vs. alliances against,
    150
  coalitions vs., 149–50
  proposal of, in offer of denied
    coalition, 151
  use of, for avoiding denied
    coalition, 154, 155
analogic communication, 73, 89
  seating arrangements as, 93–94,
    96, 106–7
  working groups for study of,
    100–103
  see also nonverbal communication
Anolli, Luigi, 125–38
Ashby, W. R., 133, 140

assimilation, 137
authoritarian behavior, 99, 100,
    132

Bateson, G., vii, xii, xiv, 57, 58,
    130–32, 137–38, 153
Battacchi, M. W., 136
Beavin, J. H., 161, 164
Beer, S., 49
behavioral communication, 73,
    92–93, 95–96
Bowlby, J., 55, 56
Buckley, W., 139–40

character, 132
clients, identification of, 42–43
coalitions, 7, 12, 13, 22–23, 41, 87,
    115, 117, 118–19, 120, 125
  alliances vs., 149–50

185

Mara Selvini Palazzoli is recognized worldwide as an authority on family systems and family therapy, and is widely published in the United States in such journals as *Family Process* and the *Journal of Marital and Family Therapy.* The other contributors, all of them psychologists, are members of a group formed in 1972 specifically to study behavior in large organizations, which led to the writing of this book.